C-2211   CAREER EXAMINATION SERIES

*This is your
PASSBOOK for...*

Postal Police Officer (USPS)

**Test Preparation Study Guide
Questions & Answers**

NATIONAL LEARNING CORPORATION®

COPYRIGHT NOTICE

This book is SOLELY intended for, is sold ONLY to, and its use is RESTRICTED to individual, bona fide applicants or candidates who qualify by virtue of having seriously filed applications for appropriate license, certificate, professional and/or promotional advancement, higher school matriculation, scholarship, or other legitimate requirements of education and/or governmental authorities.

This book is NOT intended for use, class instruction, tutoring, training, duplication, copying, reprinting, excerption, or adaptation, etc., by:

1) Other publishers
2) Proprietors and/or Instructors of "Coaching" and/or Preparatory Courses
3) Personnel and/or Training Divisions of commercial, industrial, and governmental organizations
4) Schools, colleges, or universities and/or their departments and staffs, including teachers and other personnel
5) Testing Agencies or Bureaus
6) Study groups which seek by the purchase of a single volume to copy and/or duplicate and/or adapt this material for use by the group as a whole without having purchased individual volumes for each of the members of the group
7) Et al.

Such persons would be in violation of appropriate Federal and State statutes.

PROVISION OF LICENSING AGREEMENTS – Recognized educational, commercial, industrial, and governmental institutions and organizations, and others legitimately engaged in educational pursuits, including training, testing, and measurement activities, may address request for a licensing agreement to the copyright owners, who will determine whether, and under what conditions, including fees and charges, the materials in this book may be used them. In other words, a licensing facility exists for the legitimate use of the material in this book on other than an individual basis. However, it is asseverated and affirmed here that the material in this book CANNOT be used without the receipt of the express permission of such a licensing agreement from the Publishers. Inquiries re licensing should be addressed to the company, attention rights and permissions department.

All rights reserved, including the right of reproduction in whole or in part, in any form or by any means, electronic or mechanical, including photocopying, recording, or by any information storage and retrieval system, without permission in writing from the Publisher.

Copyright © 2024 by
National Learning Corporation

212 Michael Drive, Syosset, NY 11791
(516) 921-8888 • www.passbooks.com
E-mail: info@passbooks.com

PUBLISHED IN THE UNITED STATES OF AMERICA

PASSBOOK® SERIES

THE *PASSBOOK® SERIES* has been created to prepare applicants and candidates for the ultimate academic battlefield – the examination room.

At some time in our lives, each and every one of us may be required to take an examination – for validation, matriculation, admission, qualification, registration, certification, or licensure.

Based on the assumption that every applicant or candidate has met the basic formal educational standards, has taken the required number of courses, and read the necessary texts, the *PASSBOOK® SERIES* furnishes the one special preparation which may assure passing with confidence, instead of failing with insecurity. Examination questions – together with answers – are furnished as the basic vehicle for study so that the mysteries of the examination and its compounding difficulties may be eliminated or diminished by a sure method.

This book is meant to help you pass your examination provided that you qualify and are serious in your objective.

The entire field is reviewed through the huge store of content information which is succinctly presented through a provocative and challenging approach – the question-and-answer method.

A climate of success is established by furnishing the correct answers at the end of each test.

You soon learn to recognize types of questions, forms of questions, and patterns of questioning. You may even begin to anticipate expected outcomes.

You perceive that many questions are repeated or adapted so that you can gain acute insights, which may enable you to score many sure points.

You learn how to confront new questions, or types of questions, and to attack them confidently and work out the correct answers.

You note objectives and emphases, and recognize pitfalls and dangers, so that you may make positive educational adjustments.

Moreover, you are kept fully informed in relation to new concepts, methods, practices, and directions in the field.

You discover that you are actually taking the examination all the time: you are preparing for the examination by "taking" an examination, not by reading extraneous and/or supererogatory textbooks.

In short, this PASSBOOK®, used directedly, should be an important factor in helping you to pass your test.

POSTAL POLICE OFFICER

DUTIES:
Postal Police Officers perform duties on postal property. They prevent depredation, loss or damage of postal property and mail, on postal property. They patrol and observe postal premises to prevent assaults on postal employees. They monitor persons in and around postal property and act to prevent prohibited items from being brought on postal premises, and they confiscate such items. They operate motor vehicles and monitor electronic security devices that provide surveillance and alarm, vehicles and they immediately respond to emergent situations including accidents, illness, lire, unrest and other circumstances threatening life and property. They carry a firearm in the exercise of their duties. They may be required to work hours outside assigned tour.

GENERAL QUALIFICATION
This position requires a sensitive security clearance.
All applicants must pass a written examination.

Applicants must possess a valid state driver license issued-in the state in which they reside and have a safe driving record for two (2) years or more.
Applicants must be at least 21 years of age.
Applicants must be citizens of the United States of America. Verification is required.
Applicants (if not currently an Inspection Service employee) must pass a drug screening test.
Applicants who qualify on the examination and are in the area of consideration for employment will be scheduled for a drug test and a medical examination.
Applicants must be physically able to effectively perform the duties of the position. Their weight must be proportionate to their height.
Applicants must have uncorrected vision of 20/200 (Snellen) in both eyes, correctable to 20/20 in one eye and 20/40 in the other. Good color perception is essential.

HOW TO TAKE A TEST

I. YOU MUST PASS AN EXAMINATION

A. WHAT EVERY CANDIDATE SHOULD KNOW

Examination applicants often ask us for help in preparing for the written test. What can I study in advance? What kinds of questions will be asked? How will the test be given? How will the papers be graded?

As an applicant for a civil service examination, you may be wondering about some of these things. Our purpose here is to suggest effective methods of advance study and to describe civil service examinations.

Your chances for success on this examination can be increased if you know how to prepare. Those "pre-examination jitters" can be reduced if you know what to expect. You can even experience an adventure in good citizenship if you know why civil service exams are given.

B. WHY ARE CIVIL SERVICE EXAMINATIONS GIVEN?

Civil service examinations are important to you in two ways. As a citizen, you want public jobs filled by employees who know how to do their work. As a job seeker, you want a fair chance to compete for that job on an equal footing with other candidates. The best-known means of accomplishing this two-fold goal is the competitive examination.

Exams are widely publicized throughout the nation. They may be administered for jobs in federal, state, city, municipal, town or village governments or agencies.

Any citizen may apply, with some limitations, such as the age or residence of applicants. Your experience and education may be reviewed to see whether you meet the requirements for the particular examination. When these requirements exist, they are reasonable and applied consistently to all applicants. Thus, a competitive examination may cause you some uneasiness now, but it is your privilege and safeguard.

C. HOW ARE CIVIL SERVICE EXAMS DEVELOPED?

Examinations are carefully written by trained technicians who are specialists in the field known as "psychological measurement," in consultation with recognized authorities in the field of work that the test will cover. These experts recommend the subject matter areas or skills to be tested; only those knowledges or skills important to your success on the job are included. The most reliable books and source materials available are used as references. Together, the experts and technicians judge the difficulty level of the questions.

Test technicians know how to phrase questions so that the problem is clearly stated. Their ethics do not permit "trick" or "catch" questions. Questions may have been tried out on sample groups, or subjected to statistical analysis, to determine their usefulness.

Written tests are often used in combination with performance tests, ratings of training and experience, and oral interviews. All of these measures combine to form the best-known means of finding the right person for the right job.

II. HOW TO PASS THE WRITTEN TEST

A. NATURE OF THE EXAMINATION

To prepare intelligently for civil service examinations, you should know how they differ from school examinations you have taken. In school you were assigned certain definite pages to read or subjects to cover. The examination questions were quite detailed and usually emphasized memory. Civil service exams, on the other hand, try to discover your present ability to perform the duties of a position, plus your potentiality to learn these duties. In other words, a civil service exam attempts to predict how successful you will be. Questions cover such a broad area that they cannot be as minute and detailed as school exam questions.

In the public service similar kinds of work, or positions, are grouped together in one "class." This process is known as *position-classification*. All the positions in a class are paid according to the salary range for that class. One class title covers all of these positions, and they are all tested by the same examination.

B. FOUR BASIC STEPS

1) Study the announcement

How, then, can you know what subjects to study? Our best answer is: "Learn as much as possible about the class of positions for which you've applied." The exam will test the knowledge, skills and abilities needed to do the work.

Your most valuable source of information about the position you want is the official exam announcement. This announcement lists the training and experience qualifications. Check these standards and apply only if you come reasonably close to meeting them.

The brief description of the position in the examination announcement offers some clues to the subjects which will be tested. Think about the job itself. Review the duties in your mind. Can you perform them, or are there some in which you are rusty? Fill in the blank spots in your preparation.

Many jurisdictions preview the written test in the exam announcement by including a section called "Knowledge and Abilities Required," "Scope of the Examination," or some similar heading. Here you will find out specifically what fields will be tested.

2) Review your own background

Once you learn in general what the position is all about, and what you need to know to do the work, ask yourself which subjects you already know fairly well and which need improvement. You may wonder whether to concentrate on improving your strong areas or on building some background in your fields of weakness. When the announcement has specified "some knowledge" or "considerable knowledge," or has used adjectives like "beginning principles of..." or "advanced ... methods," you can get a clue as to the number and difficulty of questions to be asked in any given field. More questions, and hence broader coverage, would be included for those subjects which are more important in the work. Now weigh your strengths and weaknesses against the job requirements and prepare accordingly.

3) Determine the level of the position

Another way to tell how intensively you should prepare is to understand the level of the job for which you are applying. Is it the entering level? In other words, is this the position in which beginners in a field of work are hired? Or is it an intermediate or advanced level? Sometimes this is indicated by such words as "Junior" or "Senior" in the class title. Other jurisdictions use Roman numerals to designate the level – Clerk I, Clerk II, for example. The word "Supervisor" sometimes appears in the title. If the level is not indicated by the title, check the description of duties. Will you be working under very close supervision, or will you have responsibility for independent decisions in this work?

4) Choose appropriate study materials

Now that you know the subjects to be examined and the relative amount of each subject to be covered, you can choose suitable study materials. For beginning level jobs, or even advanced ones, if you have a pronounced weakness in some aspect of your training, read a modern, standard textbook in that field. Be sure it is up to date and has general coverage. Such books are normally available at your library, and the librarian will be glad to help you locate one. For entry-level positions, questions of appropriate difficulty are chosen – neither highly advanced questions, nor those too simple. Such questions require careful thought but not advanced training.

If the position for which you are applying is technical or advanced, you will read more advanced, specialized material. If you are already familiar with the basic principles of your field, elementary textbooks would waste your time. Concentrate on advanced textbooks and technical periodicals. Think through the concepts and review difficult problems in your field.

These are all general sources. You can get more ideas on your own initiative, following these leads. For example, training manuals and publications of the government agency which employs workers in your field can be useful, particularly for technical and professional positions. A letter or visit to the government department involved may result in more specific study suggestions, and certainly will provide you with a more definite idea of the exact nature of the position you are seeking.

III. KINDS OF TESTS

Tests are used for purposes other than measuring knowledge and ability to perform specified duties. For some positions, it is equally important to test ability to make adjustments to new situations or to profit from training. In others, basic mental abilities not dependent on information are essential. Questions which test these things may not appear as pertinent to the duties of the position as those which test for knowledge and information. Yet they are often highly important parts of a fair examination. For very general questions, it is almost impossible to help you direct your study efforts. What we can do is to point out some of the more common of these general abilities needed in public service positions and describe some typical questions.

1) General information

Broad, general information has been found useful for predicting job success in some kinds of work. This is tested in a variety of ways, from vocabulary lists to questions about current events. Basic background in some field of work, such as sociology or economics, may be sampled in a group of questions. Often these are principles which have become familiar to most persons through exposure rather than through formal training. It is difficult to advise you how to study for these questions; being alert to the world around you is our best suggestion.

2) Verbal ability

An example of an ability needed in many positions is verbal or language ability. Verbal ability is, in brief, the ability to use and understand words. Vocabulary and grammar tests are typical measures of this ability. Reading comprehension or paragraph interpretation questions are common in many kinds of civil service tests. You are given a paragraph of written material and asked to find its central meaning.

3) Numerical ability

Number skills can be tested by the familiar arithmetic problem, by checking paired lists of numbers to see which are alike and which are different, or by interpreting charts and graphs. In the latter test, a graph may be printed in the test booklet which you are asked to use as the basis for answering questions.

4) Observation

A popular test for law-enforcement positions is the observation test. A picture is shown to you for several minutes, then taken away. Questions about the picture test your ability to observe both details and larger elements.

5) Following directions

In many positions in the public service, the employee must be able to carry out written instructions dependably and accurately. You may be given a chart with several columns, each column listing a variety of information. The questions require you to carry out directions involving the information given in the chart.

6) Skills and aptitudes

Performance tests effectively measure some manual skills and aptitudes. When the skill is one in which you are trained, such as typing or shorthand, you can practice. These tests are often very much like those given in business school or high school courses. For many of the other skills and aptitudes, however, no short-time preparation can be made. Skills and abilities natural to you or that you have developed throughout your lifetime are being tested.

Many of the general questions just described provide all the data needed to answer the questions and ask you to use your reasoning ability to find the answers. Your best preparation for these tests, as well as for tests of facts and ideas, is to be at your physical and mental best. You, no doubt, have your own methods of getting into an exam-taking mood and keeping "in shape." The next section lists some ideas on this subject.

IV. KINDS OF QUESTIONS

Only rarely is the "essay" question, which you answer in narrative form, used in civil service tests. Civil service tests are usually of the short-answer type. Full instructions for answering these questions will be given to you at the examination. But in case this is your first experience with short-answer questions and separate answer sheets, here is what you need to know:

1) Multiple-choice Questions

Most popular of the short-answer questions is the "multiple choice" or "best answer" question. It can be used, for example, to test for factual knowledge, ability to solve problems or judgment in meeting situations found at work.

A multiple-choice question is normally one of three types—
- It can begin with an incomplete statement followed by several possible endings. You are to find the one ending which *best* completes the statement, although some of the others may not be entirely wrong.
- It can also be a complete statement in the form of a question which is answered by choosing one of the statements listed.

- It can be in the form of a problem – again you select the best answer.

Here is an example of a multiple-choice question with a discussion which should give you some clues as to the method for choosing the right answer:

When an employee has a complaint about his assignment, the action which will *best* help him overcome his difficulty is to
   A. discuss his difficulty with his coworkers
   B. take the problem to the head of the organization
   C. take the problem to the person who gave him the assignment
   D. say nothing to anyone about his complaint

In answering this question, you should study each of the choices to find which is best. Consider choice "A" – Certainly an employee may discuss his complaint with fellow employees, but no change or improvement can result, and the complaint remains unresolved. Choice "B" is a poor choice since the head of the organization probably does not know what assignment you have been given, and taking your problem to him is known as "going over the head" of the supervisor. The supervisor, or person who made the assignment, is the person who can clarify it or correct any injustice. Choice "C" is, therefore, correct. To say nothing, as in choice "D," is unwise. Supervisors have and interest in knowing the problems employees are facing, and the employee is seeking a solution to his problem.

2) True/False Questions

The "true/false" or "right/wrong" form of question is sometimes used. Here a complete statement is given. Your job is to decide whether the statement is right or wrong.

SAMPLE: A roaming cell-phone call to a nearby city costs less than a non-roaming call to a distant city.

This statement is wrong, or false, since roaming calls are more expensive.

This is not a complete list of all possible question forms, although most of the others are variations of these common types. You will always get complete directions for answering questions. Be sure you understand *how* to mark your answers – ask questions until you do.

V. RECORDING YOUR ANSWERS

Computer terminals are used more and more today for many different kinds of exams.
For an examination with very few applicants, you may be told to record your answers in the test booklet itself. Separate answer sheets are much more common. If this separate answer sheet is to be scored by machine – and this is often the case – it is highly important that you mark your answers correctly in order to get credit.
An electronic scoring machine is often used in civil service offices because of the speed with which papers can be scored. Machine-scored answer sheets must be marked with a pencil, which will be given to you. This pencil has a high graphite content which responds to the electronic scoring machine. As a matter of fact, stray dots may register as answers, so do not let your pencil rest on the answer sheet while you are pondering the correct answer. Also, if your pencil lead breaks or is otherwise defective, ask for another.

Since the answer sheet will be dropped in a slot in the scoring machine, be careful not to bend the corners or get the paper crumpled.

The answer sheet normally has five vertical columns of numbers, with 30 numbers to a column. These numbers correspond to the question numbers in your test booklet. After each number, going across the page are four or five pairs of dotted lines. These short dotted lines have small letters or numbers above them. The first two pairs may also have a "T" or "F" above the letters. This indicates that the first two pairs only are to be used if the questions are of the true-false type. If the questions are multiple choice, disregard the "T" and "F" and pay attention only to the small letters or numbers.

Answer your questions in the manner of the sample that follows:

32. The largest city in the United States is
    A. Washington, D.C.
    B. New York City
    C. Chicago
    D. Detroit
    E. San Francisco

1) Choose the answer you think is best. (New York City is the largest, so "B" is correct.)
2) Find the row of dotted lines numbered the same as the question you are answering. (Find row number 32)
3) Find the pair of dotted lines corresponding to the answer. (Find the pair of lines under the mark "B.")
4) Make a solid black mark between the dotted lines.

VI. BEFORE THE TEST

Common sense will help you find procedures to follow to get ready for an examination. Too many of us, however, overlook these sensible measures. Indeed, nervousness and fatigue have been found to be the most serious reasons why applicants fail to do their best on civil service tests. Here is a list of reminders:

- Begin your preparation early – Don't wait until the last minute to go scurrying around for books and materials or to find out what the position is all about.
- Prepare continuously – An hour a night for a week is better than an all-night cram session. This has been definitely established. What is more, a night a week for a month will return better dividends than crowding your study into a shorter period of time.
- Locate the place of the exam – You have been sent a notice telling you when and where to report for the examination. If the location is in a different town or otherwise unfamiliar to you, it would be well to inquire the best route and learn something about the building.
- Relax the night before the test – Allow your mind to rest. Do not study at all that night. Plan some mild recreation or diversion; then go to bed early and get a good night's sleep.
- Get up early enough to make a leisurely trip to the place for the test – This way unforeseen events, traffic snarls, unfamiliar buildings, etc. will not upset you.
- Dress comfortably – A written test is not a fashion show. You will be known by number and not by name, so wear something comfortable.

- Leave excess paraphernalia at home – Shopping bags and odd bundles will get in your way. You need bring only the items mentioned in the official notice you received; usually everything you need is provided. Do not bring reference books to the exam. They will only confuse those last minutes and be taken away from you when in the test room.
- Arrive somewhat ahead of time – If because of transportation schedules you must get there very early, bring a newspaper or magazine to take your mind off yourself while waiting.
- Locate the examination room – When you have found the proper room, you will be directed to the seat or part of the room where you will sit. Sometimes you are given a sheet of instructions to read while you are waiting. Do not fill out any forms until you are told to do so; just read them and be prepared.
- Relax and prepare to listen to the instructions
- If you have any physical problem that may keep you from doing your best, be sure to tell the test administrator. If you are sick or in poor health, you really cannot do your best on the exam. You can come back and take the test some other time.

VII. AT THE TEST

The day of the test is here and you have the test booklet in your hand. The temptation to get going is very strong. Caution! There is more to success than knowing the right answers. You must know how to identify your papers and understand variations in the type of short-answer question used in this particular examination. Follow these suggestions for maximum results from your efforts:

1) Cooperate with the monitor

The test administrator has a duty to create a situation in which you can be as much at ease as possible. He will give instructions, tell you when to begin, check to see that you are marking your answer sheet correctly, and so on. He is not there to guard you, although he will see that your competitors do not take unfair advantage. He wants to help you do your best.

2) Listen to all instructions

Don't jump the gun! Wait until you understand all directions. In most civil service tests you get more time than you need to answer the questions. So don't be in a hurry. Read each word of instructions until you clearly understand the meaning. Study the examples, listen to all announcements and follow directions. Ask questions if you do not understand what to do.

3) Identify your papers

Civil service exams are usually identified by number only. You will be assigned a number; you must not put your name on your test papers. Be sure to copy your number correctly. Since more than one exam may be given, copy your exact examination title.

4) Plan your time

Unless you are told that a test is a "speed" or "rate of work" test, speed itself is usually not important. Time enough to answer all the questions will be provided, but this does not mean that you have all day. An overall time limit has been set. Divide the total time (in minutes) by the number of questions to determine the approximate time you have for each question.

5) Do not linger over difficult questions

If you come across a difficult question, mark it with a paper clip (useful to have along) and come back to it when you have been through the booklet. One caution if you do this – be sure to skip a number on your answer sheet as well. Check often to be sure that you have not lost your place and that you are marking in the row numbered the same as the question you are answering.

6) Read the questions

Be sure you know what the question asks! Many capable people are unsuccessful because they failed to *read* the questions correctly.

7) Answer all questions

Unless you have been instructed that a penalty will be deducted for incorrect answers, it is better to guess than to omit a question.

8) Speed tests

It is often better NOT to guess on speed tests. It has been found that on timed tests people are tempted to spend the last few seconds before time is called in marking answers at random – without even reading them – in the hope of picking up a few extra points. To discourage this practice, the instructions may warn you that your score will be "corrected" for guessing. That is, a penalty will be applied. The incorrect answers will be deducted from the correct ones, or some other penalty formula will be used.

9) Review your answers

If you finish before time is called, go back to the questions you guessed or omitted to give them further thought. Review other answers if you have time.

10) Return your test materials

If you are ready to leave before others have finished or time is called, take ALL your materials to the monitor and leave quietly. Never take any test material with you. The monitor can discover whose papers are not complete, and taking a test booklet may be grounds for disqualification.

VIII. EXAMINATION TECHNIQUES

1) Read the general instructions carefully. These are usually printed on the first page of the exam booklet. As a rule, these instructions refer to the timing of the examination; the fact that you should not start work until the signal and must stop work at a signal, etc. If there are any *special* instructions, such as a choice of questions to be answered, make sure that you note this instruction carefully.

2) When you are ready to start work on the examination, that is as soon as the signal has been given, read the instructions to each question booklet, underline any key words or phrases, such as *least, best, outline, describe* and the like. In this way you will tend to answer as requested rather than discover on reviewing your paper that you *listed without describing*, that you selected the *worst* choice rather than the *best* choice, etc.

3) If the examination is of the objective or multiple-choice type – that is, each question will also give a series of possible answers: A, B, C or D, and you are called upon to select the best answer and write the letter next to that answer on your answer paper – it is advisable to start answering each question in turn. There may be anywhere from 50 to 100 such questions in the three or four hours allotted and you can see how much time would be taken if you read through all the questions before beginning to answer any. Furthermore, if you come across a question or group of questions which you know would be difficult to answer, it would undoubtedly affect your handling of all the other questions.

4) If the examination is of the essay type and contains but a few questions, it is a moot point as to whether you should read all the questions before starting to answer any one. Of course, if you are given a choice – say five out of seven and the like – then it is essential to read all the questions so you can eliminate the two that are most difficult. If, however, you are asked to answer all the questions, there may be danger in trying to answer the easiest one first because you may find that you will spend too much time on it. The best technique is to answer the first question, then proceed to the second, etc.

5) Time your answers. Before the exam begins, write down the time it started, then add the time allowed for the examination and write down the time it must be completed, then divide the time available somewhat as follows:
   - If 3-1/2 hours are allowed, that would be 210 minutes. If you have 80 objective-type questions, that would be an average of 2-1/2 minutes per question. Allow yourself no more than 2 minutes per question, or a total of 160 minutes, which will permit about 50 minutes to review.
   - If for the time allotment of 210 minutes there are 7 essay questions to answer, that would average about 30 minutes a question. Give yourself only 25 minutes per question so that you have about 35 minutes to review.

6) The most important instruction is to *read each question* and make sure you know what is wanted. The second most important instruction is to *time yourself properly* so that you answer every question. The third most important instruction is to *answer every question*. Guess if you have to but include something for each question. Remember that you will receive no credit for a blank and will probably receive some credit if you write something in answer to an essay question. If you guess a letter – say "B" for a multiple-choice question – you may have guessed right. If you leave a blank as an answer to a multiple-choice question, the examiners may respect your feelings but it will not add a point to your score. Some exams may penalize you for wrong answers, so in such cases *only*, you may not want to guess unless you have some basis for your answer.

7) Suggestions
   a. Objective-type questions
      1. Examine the question booklet for proper sequence of pages and questions
      2. Read all instructions carefully
      3. Skip any question which seems too difficult; return to it after all other questions have been answered
      4. Apportion your time properly; do not spend too much time on any single question or group of questions

5. Note and underline key words – *all, most, fewest, least, best, worst, same, opposite,* etc.
6. Pay particular attention to negatives
7. Note unusual option, e.g., unduly long, short, complex, different or similar in content to the body of the question
8. Observe the use of "hedging" words – *probably, may, most likely,* etc.
9. Make sure that your answer is put next to the same number as the question
10. Do not second-guess unless you have good reason to believe the second answer is definitely more correct
11. Cross out original answer if you decide another answer is more accurate; do not erase until you are ready to hand your paper in
12. Answer all questions; guess unless instructed otherwise
13. Leave time for review

  b. Essay questions
     1. Read each question carefully
     2. Determine exactly what is wanted. Underline key words or phrases.
     3. Decide on outline or paragraph answer
     4. Include many different points and elements unless asked to develop any one or two points or elements
     5. Show impartiality by giving pros and cons unless directed to select one side only
     6. Make and write down any assumptions you find necessary to answer the questions
     7. Watch your English, grammar, punctuation and choice of words
     8. Time your answers; don't crowd material

8) Answering the essay question

Most essay questions can be answered by framing the specific response around several key words or ideas. Here are a few such key words or ideas:

M's: manpower, materials, methods, money, management
P's: purpose, program, policy, plan, procedure, practice, problems, pitfalls, personnel, public relations

  a. Six basic steps in handling problems:
     1. Preliminary plan and background development
     2. Collect information, data and facts
     3. Analyze and interpret information, data and facts
     4. Analyze and develop solutions as well as make recommendations
     5. Prepare report and sell recommendations
     6. Install recommendations and follow up effectiveness

  b. Pitfalls to avoid
     1. *Taking things for granted* – A statement of the situation does not necessarily imply that each of the elements is necessarily true; for example, a complaint may be invalid and biased so that all that can be taken for granted is that a complaint has been registered

2. *Considering only one side of a situation* – Wherever possible, indicate several alternatives and then point out the reasons you selected the best one
3. *Failing to indicate follow up* – Whenever your answer indicates action on your part, make certain that you will take proper follow-up action to see how successful your recommendations, procedures or actions turn out to be
4. *Taking too long in answering any single question* – Remember to time your answers properly

IX. AFTER THE TEST

Scoring procedures differ in detail among civil service jurisdictions although the general principles are the same. Whether the papers are hand-scored or graded by machine we have described, they are nearly always graded by number. That is, the person who marks the paper knows only the number – never the name – of the applicant. Not until all the papers have been graded will they be matched with names. If other tests, such as training and experience or oral interview ratings have been given, scores will be combined. Different parts of the examination usually have different weights. For example, the written test might count 60 percent of the final grade, and a rating of training and experience 40 percent. In many jurisdictions, veterans will have a certain number of points added to their grades.

After the final grade has been determined, the names are placed in grade order and an eligible list is established. There are various methods for resolving ties between those who get the same final grade – probably the most common is to place first the name of the person whose application was received first. Job offers are made from the eligible list in the order the names appear on it. You will be notified of your grade and your rank as soon as all these computations have been made. This will be done as rapidly as possible.

People who are found to meet the requirements in the announcement are called "eligibles." Their names are put on a list of eligible candidates. An eligible's chances of getting a job depend on how high he stands on this list and how fast agencies are filling jobs from the list.

When a job is to be filled from a list of eligibles, the agency asks for the names of people on the list of eligibles for that job. When the civil service commission receives this request, it sends to the agency the names of the three people highest on this list. Or, if the job to be filled has specialized requirements, the office sends the agency the names of the top three persons who meet these requirements from the general list.

The appointing officer makes a choice from among the three people whose names were sent to him. If the selected person accepts the appointment, the names of the others are put back on the list to be considered for future openings.

That is the rule in hiring from all kinds of eligible lists, whether they are for typist, carpenter, chemist, or something else. For every vacancy, the appointing officer has his choice of any one of the top three eligibles on the list. This explains why the person whose name is on top of the list sometimes does not get an appointment when some of the persons lower on the list do. If the appointing officer chooses the second or third eligible, the No. 1 eligible does not get a job at once, but stays on the list until he is appointed or the list is terminated.

X. HOW TO PASS THE INTERVIEW TEST

The examination for which you applied requires an oral interview test. You have already taken the written test and you are now being called for the interview test – the final part of the formal examination.

You may think that it is not possible to prepare for an interview test and that there are no procedures to follow during an interview. Our purpose is to point out some things you can do in advance that will help you and some good rules to follow and pitfalls to avoid while you are being interviewed.

What is an interview supposed to test?

The written examination is designed to test the technical knowledge and competence of the candidate; the oral is designed to evaluate intangible qualities, not readily measured otherwise, and to establish a list showing the relative fitness of each candidate – as measured against his competitors – for the position sought. Scoring is not on the basis of "right" and "wrong," but on a sliding scale of values ranging from "not passable" to "outstanding." As a matter of fact, it is possible to achieve a relatively low score without a single "incorrect" answer because of evident weakness in the qualities being measured.

Occasionally, an examination may consist entirely of an oral test – either an individual or a group oral. In such cases, information is sought concerning the technical knowledges and abilities of the candidate, since there has been no written examination for this purpose. More commonly, however, an oral test is used to supplement a written examination.

Who conducts interviews?

The composition of oral boards varies among different jurisdictions. In nearly all, a representative of the personnel department serves as chairman. One of the members of the board may be a representative of the department in which the candidate would work. In some cases, "outside experts" are used, and, frequently, a businessman or some other representative of the general public is asked to serve. Labor and management or other special groups may be represented. The aim is to secure the services of experts in the appropriate field.

However the board is composed, it is a good idea (and not at all improper or unethical) to ascertain in advance of the interview who the members are and what groups they represent. When you are introduced to them, you will have some idea of their backgrounds and interests, and at least you will not stutter and stammer over their names.

What should be done before the interview?

While knowledge about the board members is useful and takes some of the surprise element out of the interview, there is other preparation which is more substantive. It *is* possible to prepare for an oral interview – in several ways:

1) Keep a copy of your application and review it carefully before the interview

This may be the only document before the oral board, and the starting point of the interview. Know what education and experience you have listed there, and the sequence and dates of all of it. Sometimes the board will ask you to review the highlights of your experience for them; you should not have to hem and haw doing it.

2) Study the class specification and the examination announcement

Usually, the oral board has one or both of these to guide them. The qualities, characteristics or knowledges required by the position sought are stated in these documents. They offer valuable clues as to the nature of the oral interview. For example, if the job involves supervisory responsibilities, the announcement will usually indicate that knowledge of modern supervisory methods and the qualifications of the candidate as a supervisor will be tested. If so, you can expect such questions, frequently in the form of a hypothetical situation which you are expected to solve. NEVER go into an oral without knowledge of the duties and responsibilities of the job you seek.

3) Think through each qualification required

Try to visualize the kind of questions you would ask if you were a board member. How well could you answer them? Try especially to appraise your own knowledge and background in each area, *measured against the job sought*, and identify any areas in which you are weak. Be critical and realistic – do not flatter yourself.

4) Do some general reading in areas in which you feel you may be weak

For example, if the job involves supervision and your past experience has NOT, some general reading in supervisory methods and practices, particularly in the field of human relations, might be useful. Do NOT study agency procedures or detailed manuals. The oral board will be testing your understanding and capacity, not your memory.

5) Get a good night's sleep and watch your general health and mental attitude

You will want a clear head at the interview. Take care of a cold or any other minor ailment, and of course, no hangovers.

What should be done on the day of the interview?

Now comes the day of the interview itself. Give yourself plenty of time to get there. Plan to arrive somewhat ahead of the scheduled time, particularly if your appointment is in the fore part of the day. If a previous candidate fails to appear, the board might be ready for you a bit early. By early afternoon an oral board is almost invariably behind schedule if there are many candidates, and you may have to wait. Take along a book or magazine to read, or your application to review, but leave any extraneous material in the waiting room when you go in for your interview. In any event, relax and compose yourself.

The matter of dress is important. The board is forming impressions about you – from your experience, your manners, your attitude, and your appearance. Give your personal appearance careful attention. Dress your best, but not your flashiest. Choose conservative, appropriate clothing, and be sure it is immaculate. This is a business interview, and your appearance should indicate that you regard it as such. Besides, being well groomed and properly dressed will help boost your confidence.

Sooner or later, someone will call your name and escort you into the interview room. *This is it.* From here on you are on your own. It is too late for any more preparation. But remember, you asked for this opportunity to prove your fitness, and you are here because your request was granted.

What happens when you go in?

The usual sequence of events will be as follows: The clerk (who is often the board stenographer) will introduce you to the chairman of the oral board, who will introduce you to the other members of the board. Acknowledge the introductions before you sit down. Do not be surprised if you find a microphone facing you or a stenotypist sitting by. Oral interviews are usually recorded in the event of an appeal or other review.

Usually the chairman of the board will open the interview by reviewing the highlights of your education and work experience from your application – primarily for the benefit of the other members of the board, as well as to get the material into the record. Do not interrupt or comment unless there is an error or significant misinterpretation; if that is the case, do not hesitate. But do not quibble about insignificant matters. Also, he will usually ask you some question about your education, experience or your present job – partly to get you to start talking and to establish the interviewing "rapport." He may start the actual questioning, or turn it over to one of the other members. Frequently, each member undertakes the questioning on a particular area, one in which he is perhaps most competent, so you can expect each member to participate in the examination. Because time is limited, you may also expect some rather abrupt switches in the direction the questioning takes, so do not be upset by it. Normally, a board member will not pursue a single line of questioning unless he discovers a particular strength or weakness.

After each member has participated, the chairman will usually ask whether any member has any further questions, then will ask you if you have anything you wish to add. Unless you are expecting this question, it may floor you. Worse, it may start you off on an extended, extemporaneous speech. The board is not usually seeking more information. The question is principally to offer you a last opportunity to present further qualifications or to indicate that you have nothing to add. So, if you feel that a significant qualification or characteristic has been overlooked, it is proper to point it out in a sentence or so. Do not compliment the board on the thoroughness of their examination – they have been sketchy, and you know it. If you wish, merely say, "No thank you, I have nothing further to add." This is a point where you can "talk yourself out" of a good impression or fail to present an important bit of information. Remember, *you close the interview yourself*.

The chairman will then say, "That is all, Mr. _____, thank you." Do not be startled; the interview is over, and quicker than you think. Thank him, gather your belongings and take your leave. Save your sigh of relief for the other side of the door.

How to put your best foot forward

Throughout this entire process, you may feel that the board individually and collectively is trying to pierce your defenses, seek out your hidden weaknesses and embarrass and confuse you. Actually, this is not true. They are obliged to make an appraisal of your qualifications for the job you are seeking, and they want to see you in your best light. Remember, they must interview all candidates and a non-cooperative candidate may become a failure in spite of their best efforts to bring out his qualifications. Here are 15 suggestions that will help you:

1) Be natural – Keep your attitude confident, not cocky

If you are not confident that you can do the job, do not expect the board to be. Do not apologize for your weaknesses, try to bring out your strong points. The board is interested in a positive, not negative, presentation. Cockiness will antagonize any board member and make him wonder if you are covering up a weakness by a false show of strength.

2) Get comfortable, but don't lounge or sprawl

Sit erectly but not stiffly. A careless posture may lead the board to conclude that you are careless in other things, or at least that you are not impressed by the importance of the occasion. Either conclusion is natural, even if incorrect. Do not fuss with your clothing, a pencil or an ashtray. Your hands may occasionally be useful to emphasize a point; do not let them become a point of distraction.

3) Do not wisecrack or make small talk

This is a serious situation, and your attitude should show that you consider it as such. Further, the time of the board is limited – they do not want to waste it, and neither should you.

4) Do not exaggerate your experience or abilities

In the first place, from information in the application or other interviews and sources, the board may know more about you than you think. Secondly, you probably will not get away with it. An experienced board is rather adept at spotting such a situation, so do not take the chance.

5) If you know a board member, do not make a point of it, yet do not hide it

Certainly you are not fooling him, and probably not the other members of the board. Do not try to take advantage of your acquaintanceship – it will probably do you little good.

6) Do not dominate the interview

Let the board do that. They will give you the clues – do not assume that you have to do all the talking. Realize that the board has a number of questions to ask you, and do not try to take up all the interview time by showing off your extensive knowledge of the answer to the first one.

7) Be attentive

You only have 20 minutes or so, and you should keep your attention at its sharpest throughout. When a member is addressing a problem or question to you, give him your undivided attention. Address your reply principally to him, but do not exclude the other board members.

8) Do not interrupt

A board member may be stating a problem for you to analyze. He will ask you a question when the time comes. Let him state the problem, and wait for the question.

9) Make sure you understand the question

Do not try to answer until you are sure what the question is. If it is not clear, restate it in your own words or ask the board member to clarify it for you. However, do not haggle about minor elements.

10) Reply promptly but not hastily

A common entry on oral board rating sheets is "candidate responded readily," or "candidate hesitated in replies." Respond as promptly and quickly as you can, but do not jump to a hasty, ill-considered answer.

11) Do not be peremptory in your answers

A brief answer is proper – but do not fire your answer back. That is a losing game from your point of view. The board member can probably ask questions much faster than you can answer them.

12) Do not try to create the answer you think the board member wants

He is interested in what kind of mind you have and how it works – not in playing games. Furthermore, he can usually spot this practice and will actually grade you down on it.

13) Do not switch sides in your reply merely to agree with a board member

Frequently, a member will take a contrary position merely to draw you out and to see if you are willing and able to defend your point of view. Do not start a debate, yet do not surrender a good position. If a position is worth taking, it is worth defending.

14) Do not be afraid to admit an error in judgment if you are shown to be wrong

The board knows that you are forced to reply without any opportunity for careful consideration. Your answer may be demonstrably wrong. If so, admit it and get on with the interview.

15) Do not dwell at length on your present job

The opening question may relate to your present assignment. Answer the question but do not go into an extended discussion. You are being examined for a *new* job, not your present one. As a matter of fact, try to phrase ALL your answers in terms of the job for which you are being examined.

Basis of Rating

Probably you will forget most of these "do's" and "don'ts" when you walk into the oral interview room. Even remembering them all will not ensure you a passing grade. Perhaps you did not have the qualifications in the first place. But remembering them will help you to put your best foot forward, without treading on the toes of the board members.

Rumor and popular opinion to the contrary notwithstanding, an oral board wants you to make the best appearance possible. They know you are under pressure – but they also want to see how you respond to it as a guide to what your reaction would be under the pressures of the job you seek. They will be influenced by the degree of poise you display, the personal traits you show and the manner in which you respond.

ABOUT THIS BOOK

This book contains tests divided into Examination Sections. Go through each test, answering every question in the margin. We have also attached a sample answer sheet at the back of the book that can be removed and used. At the end of each test look at the answer key and check your answers. On the ones you got wrong, look at the right answer choice and learn. Do not fill in the answers first. Do not memorize the questions and answers, but understand the answer and principles involved. On your test, the questions will likely be different from the samples. Questions are changed and new ones added. If you understand these past questions you should have success with any changes that arise. Tests may consist of several types of questions. We have additional books on each subject should more study be advisable or necessary for you. Finally, the more you study, the better prepared you will be. This book is intended to be the last thing you study before you walk into the examination room. Prior study of relevant texts is also recommended. NLC publishes some of these in our Fundamental Series. Knowledge and good sense are important factors in passing your exam. Good luck also helps. So now study this Passbook, absorb the material contained within and take that knowledge into the examination. Then do your best to pass that exam.

EXAMINATION SECTION

EXAMINATION SECTION
TEST 1

DIRECTIONS: Each question or incomplete statement is followed by several suggested answers or completions. Select the one that BEST answers the question or completes the statement. *PRINT THE LETTER OF THE CORRECT ANSWER IN THE SPACE AT THE RIGHT.*

1. Of the following, the MOST important single factor in any building security program is   1.____

    A. a fool-proof employee identification system
    B. an effective control of entrances and exits
    C. bright illumination of all outside areas
    D. clearly marking public and non-public areas

2. There is general agreement that the BEST criterion of what is a good physical security system in a large public building is   2.____

    A. the number of uniformed officers needed to patrol sensitive areas
    B. how successfully the system prevents rather than detects violations
    C. the number of persons caught in the act of committing criminal offenses
    D. how successfully the system succeeds in maintaining good public relations

3. Which one of the following statements most correctly expresses the CHIEF reason why women were originally made eligible for appointment to the position of officer?   3.____

    A. Certain tasks in security protection can be performed best by assigning women.
    B. More women than men are available to fill many vacancies in this position.
    C. The government wants more women in law enforcement because of their better attendance records.
    D. Women can no longer be barred from any government jobs because of sex.

4. The MOST BASIC purpose of patrol by officers is to   4.____

    A. eliminate as much as possible the opportunity for successful misconduct
    B. investigate criminal complaints and accident cases
    C. give prompt assistance to employees and citizens in distress or requesting their help
    D. take persons into custody who commit criminal offenses against persons and property

5. The highest quality of patrol service is MOST generally obtained by   5.____

    A. frequently changing the post assignments of each officer
    B. assigning officers to posts of equal size
    C. assigning problem officers to the least desirable posts
    D. assigning the same officers to the same posts

6. The one of the following requirements which is MOST essential to the successful performance of patrol duty by individual officers is their   6.____

    A. ability to communicate effectively with higher-level officers
    B. prompt signalling according to a prescribed schedule to insure post coverages at all times

1

C. knowledge of post conditions and post hazards
D. willingness to cover large areas during periods of critical manpower shortages

7. Officers on patrol are constantly warned to be on the alert for suspicious persons, actions, and circumstances.
   With this in mind, a senior officer should emphasize the need for them to

   A. be cautious and suspicious when dealing officially with any civilian regardless of the latter's overt actions or the circumstances surrounding his dealings with the police
   B. keep looking for the unusual persons, actions, and circumstances on their posts and pay less attention to the usual
   C. take aggressive police action immediately against any unusual person or condition detected on their posts, regardless of any other circumstances
   D. become thoroughly familiar with the usual on their posts so as to be better able to detect the unusual

8. Of primary importance in the safeguarding of property from theft is a good central lock and key issuance and control system.
   Which one of the following recommendations about maintaining such a control system would be LEAST acceptable?

   A. In selecting locks to be used for the various gates, building, and storage areas, consideration should be given to the amount of security desired.
   B. Master keys should have no markings that will identify them as such and the list of holders of these keys should be frequently reviewed to determine the continuing necessity for the individuals having them.
   C. Whenever keys for outside doors or gates or for other doors which permit access to important buildings and areas are misplaced, the locks should be immediately changed or replaced pending an investigation.
   D. Whenever an employee fails to return a borrowed key at the time specified, a prompt investigation should be made by the security force.

9. In a crowded building, a fire develops in the basement, and smoke enters the crowded rooms on the first floor. Of the following, the BEST action for an officer to take after an alarm is turned in is to

   A. call out a warning that the building is on fire and that everyone should evacuate because of the immediate danger
   B. call all of the officers together for an emergency meeting and discuss a plan of action
   C. immediately call for assistance from the local police station to help in evacuating the crowd
   D. tell everyone that there is a fire in the building next door and that they should move out onto the streets through available exits

10. Which of the following is in a key position to carry out successfully a safety program of an agency? The

    A. building engineer
    B. bureau chiefs
    C. immediate supervisors
    D. public relations director

11. It is GENERALLY considered that a daily roll call inspection, which checks to see that the officers and their equipment are in good order, is

   A. *desirable,* chiefly because it informs the superior officer what men will have to purchase new uniforms within a month
   B. *desirable,* chiefly because the public forms their impressions of the organization from the appearance of the officers
   C. *undesirable,* chiefly because this kind of daily inspection unnecessarily delays officers in getting to their assigned patrol posts
   D. *undesirable,* chiefly because roll call inspection usually misses individuals reporting to work late

11._____

12. A supervising officer in giving instructions to a group of officers on the principles of accident investigation remarked, "A conclusion that appears reasonable will often be changed by exploring a factor of apparently little importance".
Which one of the following precautions does this statement emphasize as MOST important in any accident investigation?

   A. Every accident clue should be fully investigated.
   B. Accidents should not be too promptly investigated.
   C. Only specially trained officers should investigate accidents.
   D. Conclusions about accident causes are highly unreliable.

12._____

13. On a rainy day, a senior officer found that 9 of his 50 officers reported to work. What percentage of his officers was ABSENT?

   A. 18%   B. 80%   C. 82%   D. 90%

13._____

14. Officer A and Officer B work at the same post on the same days, but their hours are different. Officer A comes to work at 9:00 A.M. and leaves at 5:00 P.M., with a lunch period between 12:15 P.M. and 1:15 P.M. Officer B comes to work at 10:50 A.M. and works until 6:50 P.M., and he takes an hour for lunch between 3:00 P.M. and 4:00 P.M. What is the total amount of time between 9:00 A.M. and 6:50 P.M. that only ONE officer will be on duty?

   A. 4 hours
   B. 4 hours and 40 minutes
   C. 5 hours
   D. 5 hours and 40 minutes

14._____

15. An officer's log recorded the following attendance of 30 officers:

Monday	20	present;	10	absent
Tuesday	28	present;	2	absent
Wednesday	30	present;	0	absent
Thursday	21	present;	9	absent
Friday	16	present;	14	absent
Saturday	11	present;	19	absent
Sunday	14	present;	16	absent

   On the average, how many men were present on the weekdays (Monday - Friday)?

   A. 21   B. 23   C. 25   D. 27

15._____

16. An angry woman is being questioned by an officer when she begins shouting abuses at him.
    The BEST of the following procedures for the officer to follow is to

    A. leave the room until she has cooled off
    B. politely ignore anything she says
    C. place her under arrest by handcuffing her to a fixed object
    D. warn her that he will have to use force to restrain her making remarks

17. Of the following, which is NOT a recommended practice for an officer placing a woman offender under arrest?

    A. Assume that the offender is an innocent and virtuous person and treat her accordingly.
    B. Protect himself from attack by the woman.
    C. Refrain from using excessive physical force on the offender.
    D. Make the public aware that he is not abusing the woman.

Questions 18-21.

DIRECTIONS: Questions 18 through 21 are to be answered SOLELY on the basis of the following passage.

Specific measures for prevention of pilferage will be based on careful analysis of the conditions at each agency. The most practical and effective method to control casual pilferage is the establishment of psychological deterrents.

One of the most common means of discouraging casual pilferage is to search individuals leaving the agency at unannounced times and places. These spot searches may occasionally detect attempts at theft but greater value is realized by bringing to the attention of individuals the fact that they may be apprehended if they do attempt the illegal removal of property.

An aggressive security education program is an effective means of convincing employees that they have much more to lose than they do to gain by engaging in acts of theft. It is important for all employees to realize that pilferage is morally wrong no matter how insignificant the value of the item which is taken. In establishing any deterrent to casual pilferage, security officers must not lose sight of the fact that most employees are honest and disapprove of thievery. Mutual respect between security personnel and other employees of the agency must be maintained if the facility is to be protected from other more dangerous forms of human hazards. Any security measure which infringes on the human rights or dignity of others will jeopardize, rather than enhance, the overall protection of the agency.

18. The $100,000 yearly inventory of an agency revealed that $50 worth of goods had been stolen; the only individuals with access to the stolen materials were the employees. Of the following measures, which would the author of the preceding paragraph MOST likely recommend to a security officer?

    A. Conduct an intensive investigation of all employees to find the culprit.
    B. Make a record of the theft, but take no investigative or disciplinary action against any employee.
    C. Place a tight security check on all future movements of personnel.
    D. Remove the remainder of the material to an area with much greater security.

19. What does the passage imply is the percentage of employees whom a security officer should expect to be honest?   19.____

    A. No employee can be expected to be honest all of the time
    B. Just 50%
    C. Less than 50%
    D. More than 50%

20. According to the passage, the security officer would use which of the following methods to minimize theft in buildings with many exits when his staff is very small?   20.____

    A. Conduct an inventory of all material and place a guard near that which is most likely to be pilfered.
    B. Inform employees of the consequences of legal prosecution for pilfering.
    C. Close off the unimportant exits and have all his men concentrate on a few exits.
    D. Place a guard at each exit and conduct a casual search of individuals leaving the premises.

21. Of the following, the title BEST suited for this passage is: 21.____

    A. Control Measures for Casual Pilfering
    B. Detecting the Potential Pilferer
    C. Financial losses Resulting from Pilfering
    D. The Use of Moral Persuasion in Physical Security

22. Of the following first aid procedures, which will cause the GREATEST harm in treating a fracture?   22.____

    A. Control hemorrhages by applying direct pressure
    B. Keep the broken portion from moving about
    C. Reset a protruding bone by pressing it back into place
    D. Treat the suffering person for shock

23. During a snowstorm, a man comes to you complaining of frostbitten hands. PROPER first aid treatment in this case is to   23.____

    A. place the hands under hot running water
    B. place the hands in lukewarm water
    C. call a hospital and wait for medical aid
    D. rub the hands in melting snow

24. While on duty, an officer sees a woman apparently in a state of shock. Of the following, which one is NOT a symptom of shock?   24.____

    A. Eyes lacking luster
    B. A cold, moist forehead
    C. A shallow, irregular breathing
    D. A strong, throbbing pulse

25. You notice a man entering your building who begins coughing violently, has shortness of breath, and complains of severe chest pains. These symptoms are GENERALLY indicative of   25.____

    A. a heart attack   B. a stroke
    C. internal bleeding   D. an epileptic seizure

26. When an officer is required to record the rolled fingerprint impressions of a prisoner on the standard fingerprint form, the technique recommended by the F.B.I. as MOST likely to result in obtaining clear impressions is to roll

   A. all fingers away from the center of the prisoner's body
   B. all fingers toward the center of the prisoner's body
   C. the thumbs away from and the other fingers toward the center of the prisoner's body
   D. the thumbs toward and the other fingers away from the center of the prisoner's body

27. The principle which underlies the operation and use of a lie detector machine is that

   A. a person who is not telling the truth will be able to give a consistent story
   B. a guilty mind will unconsciously associate ideas in a very indicative manner
   C. the presence of emotional stress in a person will result in certain abnormal physical reactions
   D. many individuals are not afraid to lie

Questions 28-32.

DIRECTIONS: Questions 28 through 32 are based SOLELY on the following diagram and the paragraph preceding this group of questions. The paragraph will be divided into two statements. Statement one (1) consists of information given to the senior officer by an agency director; *this information will detail the specific security objectives the senior officer has to meet.* Statement two (2) gives the resources available to the senior officer.

NOTE: The questions are correctly answered only when all of the agency's objectives have been met and when the officer has used all his resources efficiently (i.e., to their maximum effectiveness) in meeting these objectives. All X's in the diagram indicate possible locations of officers' posts. Each X has a corresponding number which is to be used when referring to that location.

DIAGRAM

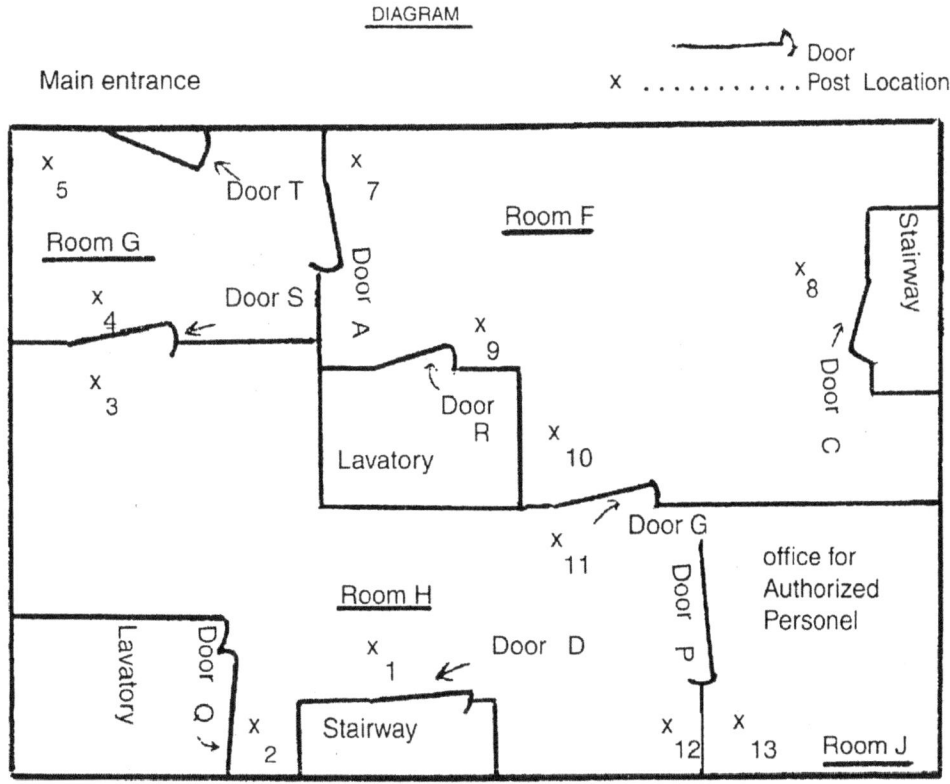

PARAGRAPH

PARAGRAPH

STATEMENT 1: Room G will be the public intake room from which persons will be directed to Room F or Room H; under no circumstances are they to enter the wrong room, and they are not to move from Room F to Room H or vice-versa. A minimum of two officers must be in each room frequented by the public at all times, and they are to keep unauthorized individuals from going to the second floor or into restricted areas. All usable entrances or exits must be covered.

STATEMENT 2: The senior officer can lock any door except the main entrance and stairway doors. He has a staff of five officers to carry out these operations.

NOTE: The senior officer is available for guard duty. Room J is an active office.

28. According to the instructions, how many officers should be assigned inside the office for authorized personnel (Room J)?

    A. 0   B. 1   C. 2   D. 3

29. In order to keep the public from moving between Room F and Room H, which door(s) can be locked without interfering with normal office operations? Door

    A. G   B. P   C. R and Q   D. S

30. When placing officers in Room H, the only way the senior officer can satisfy the agency's objectives and his manpower limitations is by placing men at locations

    A. 1 and 3   B. 1 and 12   C. 3 and 11   D. 11 and 12

31. In accordance with the instructions, the LEAST effective locations to place officers in Room F are locations

    A. 7 and 9   B. 7 and 10   C. 8 and 9   D. 9 and 10

32. In which room is it MOST difficult for each of the officers to see all the movements of the public? Room

    A. G   B. F   C. H   D. J

33. According to its own provisions, the Penal Law of the State has a number of general purposes.
    It would be LEAST accurate to state that one of these general purposes is to

    A. give fair warning of the nature of the conduct forbidden and the penalties authorized upon conviction
    B. define the act or omission and accompanying mental state which constitute each offense
    C. regulate the procedure which governs the arrest, trial and punishment of convicted offenders
    D. insure the public safety by preventing the commission of offenses through the deterrent influence of the sentences authorized upon conviction

34. Officers must be well-informed about the meaning of certain terms in connection with their enforcement duties. Which one of the following statements about such terms would be MOST accurate according to the Penal Law of the State? A(n)

    A. offense is always a crime
    B. offense is always a violation
    C. violation is never a crime
    D. felony is never an offense

35. According to the Penal Law of the State, the one of the following elements which must ALWAYS be present in order to justify the arrest of a person for criminal assault is

    A. the infliction of an actual physical injury
    B. an intent to cause an injury
    C. a threat to inflict a physical injury
    D. the use of some kind of weapon

36. A recent law of the State defines who are police officers and who are peace officers. The official title of this law is: The

    A. Criminal Code of Procedure
    B. Law of Criminal Procedure
    C. Criminal Procedure Law
    D. Code of Criminal Procedure

37. If you are required to appear in court to testify as the complainant in a criminal action, it would be MOST important for you to

    A. confine your answers to the questions asked when you are testifying
    B. help the prosecutor even if some exaggeration in your testimony may be necessary
    C. be as fair as possible to the defendant even if some details have to be omitted from your testimony
    D. avoid contradicting other witnesses testifying against the defendant

38. A senior officer is asked by the television news media to explain to the public what happened on his post during an important incident.
    When speaking with departmental permission in front of the tape recorders and cameras, the senior officer can give the MOST favorable impression of himself and his department by

    A. refusing to answer any questions but remaining calm in front of the cameras
    B. giving a detailed report of the wrong decisions made by his agency for handling the particular incident
    C. presenting the appropriate factual information in a competent way
    D. telling what should have been done during the incident and how such incidents will be handled in the future

39. Of the following suggested guidelines for officers, the one which is LEAST likely to be effective in promoting good manners and courtesy in their daily contacts with the public is:

    A. Treat inquiries by telephone in the same manner as those made in person
    B. Never look into the face of the person to whom you are speaking
    C. Never give misinformation in answer to any inquiry on a matter on which you are uncertain of the facts
    D. Show respect and consideration in both trivial and important contacts with the public

40. Assume you are an officer who has had a record of submitting late weekly reports and that you are given an order by your supervisor which is addressed to all line officers. The order states that weekly reports will be replaced by twice-weekly reports.
    The MOST logical conclusion for you to make, of the following, is:

    A. Fully detailed information was missing from your past reports
    B. Most officers have submitted late reports
    C. The supervisor needs more timely information
    D. The supervisor is attempting to punish you for your past late reports

41. A young man with long hair and "mod" clothing makes a complaint to an officer about the rudeness of another officer.
    If the senior officer is not on the premises, the officer receiving the complaint should

    A. consult with the officer who is being accused to see if the youth's story is true
    B. refer the young man to central headquarters
    C. record the complaint made against his fellow officer and ask the youth to wait until he can locate the senior officer
    D. search for the senior officer and bring him back to the site of the complainant

42. During a demonstration, which area should ALWAYS be kept clear of demonstrators? 42.____

    A. Water fountains
    B. Seating areas
    C. Doorways
    D. Restrooms

43. During demonstrations, an officer's MOST important duty is to 43.____

    A. aid the agency's employees to perform their duties
    B. promptly arrest those who might cause incidents
    C. promptly disperse the crowds of demonstrators
    D. keep the demonstrators from disrupting order

44. Of the following, what is the FIRST action a senior officer should take if a demonstration develops in his area without advance warning? 44.____

    A. Call for additional assistance from the police department
    B. Find the leaders of the demonstrators and discuss their demands
    C. See if the demonstrators intend to break the law
    D. Inform his superiors of the event taking place

45. If a senior officer is informed in the morning that a demonstration will take place during the afternoon at his assigned location, he should assemble his officers to discuss the nature and aspects of this demonstration. Of the following, the subject which it is LEAST important to discuss during this meeting is 45.____

    A. making a good impression if an officer is called before the television cameras for a personal interview
    B. the known facts and causes of the demonstration
    C. the attitude and expected behavior of the demonstrators
    D. the individual responsibilities of the officers during the demonstration

46. A male officer has probable reason to believe that a group of women occupying the ladies' toilet are using illicit drugs. 46.____
    The BEST action, of the following, for the officer to take is to

    A. call for assistance and, with the aid of such assistance, enter the toilet and escort the occupants outside
    B. ignore the situation but recommend that the ladies' toilet be closed temporarily
    C. immediately rush into the ladies' toilet and search the occupants therein
    D. knock on the door of the ladies' toilet and ask their permission to enter so that he will not be accused of trying to molest them

47. Assume that you know that a group of demonstrators will not cooperate with your request to throw handbills in a waste basket instead of on the sidewalk. You ask one of the leaders of the group, who agrees with you, to speak to the demonstrators and ask for their cooperation in this matter. 47.____
    Your request of the group leader is

    A. *desirable,* chiefly because an officer needs civilians to control the public since the officer is usually unfriendly to the views of public groups
    B. *undesirable,* chiefly because an officer should never request a civilian to perform his duties
    C. *desirable,* chiefly because the appeal of an acknowledged leader helps in gaining group cooperation

D. *undesirable,* chiefly because an institutional leader is motivated to maneuver a situation to gain his own personal advantage

48. A vague letter received from a female employee in the agency accuses an officer of improper conduct.
The initial investigative interview by the senior officer assigned to check the accusation should GENERALLY be with the

   A. accused officer
   B. female employee
   C. highest superior about disciplinary action against the officer
   D. immediate supervisor of the female employee

Questions 49-50.

DIRECTIONS: Questions 49 and 50 are to be answered SOLELY on the basis of the information in the following paragraph.

The personal conduct of each member of the Department is the primary factor in promoting desirable police-community relations. Tact, patience, and courtesy shall be strictly observed under all circumstances. A favorable public attitude toward the police must be earned; it is influenced by the personal conduct and attitude of each member of the force, by his personal integrity and courteous manner, by his respect for due process of law, by his devotion to the principles of justice, fairness, and impartiality.

49. According to the preceding paragraph, what is the BEST action an officer can take in dealing with people in a neighborhood?

   A. Assist neighborhood residents by doing favors for them.
   B. Give special attention to the community leaders in order to be able to control them effectively.
   C. Behave in an appropriate manner and give all community members the same just treatment.
   D. Prepare a plan detailing what he, the officer, wants to do for the community and submit it for approval.

50. As used in the paragraph, the word *impartiality* means *most nearly*

   A. observant   B. unbiased
   C. righteousness   D. honesty

KEY (CORRECT ANSWERS)

1. B	11. B	21. A	31. D	41. C
2. B	12. A	22. C	32. C	42. C
3. A	13. C	23. B	33. C	43. D
4. A	14. D	24. D	34. C	44. D
5. D	15. B	25. A	35. A	45. A
6. C	16. B	26. D	36. C	46. A
7. D	17. A	27. C	37. A	47. C
8. C	18. B	28. A	38. C	48. B
9. D	19. D	29. A	39. B	49. C
10. C	20. B	30. B	40. C	50. B

TEST 2

DIRECTIONS: Each question or incomplete statement is followed by several suggested answers or completions. Select the one that BEST answers the question or completes the statement. *PRINT THE LETTER OF THE CORRECT ANSWER IN THE SPACE AT THE RIGHT.*

Questions 1-5.

DIRECTIONS: Questions 1 through 5 consist of short paragraphs. Each paragraph contains one word which is INCORRECTLY used because it is NOT in keeping with the meaning of the paragraph. Find the word in each paragraph which is INCORRECTLY used, and then select as the answer the suggested word which should be substituted for the incorrectly used word.

SAMPLE QUESTION

In determining who is to do the work in your unit, you will have to decide just who does what from day to day. One of your lowest responsibilities is to assign work so that everybody gets a fair share and that everyone can do his part well.
  A. new   B. old   C. important   D. performance

EXPLANATION

The word which is NOT in keeping with the meaning of the paragraph is "lowest". This is the INCORRECTLY used word. The suggested word "important" would be in keeping with the meaning of the paragraph and should be substituted for "lowest". Therefore, the CORRECT answer is Choice C.

1. If really good practice in the elimination of preventable injuries is to be achieved and held in any establishment, top management must refuse full and definite responsibility and must apply a good share of its attention to the task.   1.____

  A. accept   B. avoidable   C. duties   D. problem

2. Recording the human face for identification is by no means the only service performed by the camera in the field of investigation. When the trial of any issue takes place, a word picture is sought to be distorted to the court of incidents, occurrences, or events which are in dispute.   2.____

  A. appeals   B. description
  C. portrayed   D. deranged

3. In the collection of physical evidence, it cannot be emphasized too strongly that a haphazard systematic search at the scene of the crime is vital. Nothing must be overlooked. Often the only leads in a case will come from the results of this search.   3.____

  A. important   B. investigation
  C. proof   D. thorough

4. If an investigator has reason to suspect that the witness is mentally stable or a habitual drunkard, he should leave no stone unturned in his investigation to determine if the witness was under the influence of liquor or drugs, or was mentally unbalanced either at the time of the occurrence to which he testified or at the time of the trial.   4.____

  A. accused   B. clue   C. deranged   D. question

13

5. The use of records is a valuable step in crime investigation and is the main reason every department should maintain accurate reports. Crimes are not committed through the use of departmental records alone but from the use of all records, of almost every type, wherever they may be found and whenever they give any incidental information regarding the criminal.

   A. accidental   B. necessary   C. reported   D. solved

Questions 6-8.

DIRECTIONS: Questions 6 through 8 are to be answered SOLELY on the basis of the following passage.

The mass media are an integral part of the daily life of virtually every American. Among these media, the youngest, television, is the most persuasive. Ninety-five percent of American homes have at least one television set, and on the average that set is in use for about 40 hours each week. The central place of television in American life makes this medium the focal point of a growing national concern over the effects of media portrayals of violence on the values, attitudes, and behavior of an ever increasing audience.

In our concern about violence and its causes, it is easy to make television a scapegoat. But we emphasise the fact that there is no simple answer to the problem of violence -- no single explanation of its causes, and no single prescription for its control. It should be remembered that America also experienced high levels of crime and violence in periods before the advent of television.

The problem of balance, taste, and artistic merit in entertaining programs on television are complex. We cannot countenance government censorship of television. Nor would we seek to impose arbitrary limitations on programming which might jeopardize television's ability to deal in dramatic presentations with controversial social issues. Nonetheless, we are deeply troubled by television's constant portrayal of violence, not in any genuine attempt to focus artistic expression on the human condition, but rather in pandering to a public preoccupation with violence that television itself has helped to generate.

6. According to the passage, television uses violence MAINLY

   A. to highlight the reality of everyday existence
   B. to satisfy the audience's hunger for destructive action
   C. to shape the values and attitudes of the public
   D. when it films documentaries concerning human conflict

7. Which one of the following statements is BEST supported by this passage?

   A. Early American history reveals a crime pattern which is not related to television.
   B. Programs should give presentations of social issues and never portray violent acts.
   C. Television has proven that entertainment programs can easily make the balance between taste and artistic merit a simple matter.
   D. Values and behavior should be regulated by governmental censorship.

8. Of the following, which word has the same meaning as countenance as it is used in the above passage?

   A. approve   B. exhibit   C. oppose   D. reject

3 (#2)

Questions 9-12.

DIRECTIONS: Questions 9 through 12 are to be answered SOLELY on the basis of the following graph relating to the burglary rate in the city, 2003 to 2008, inclusive.

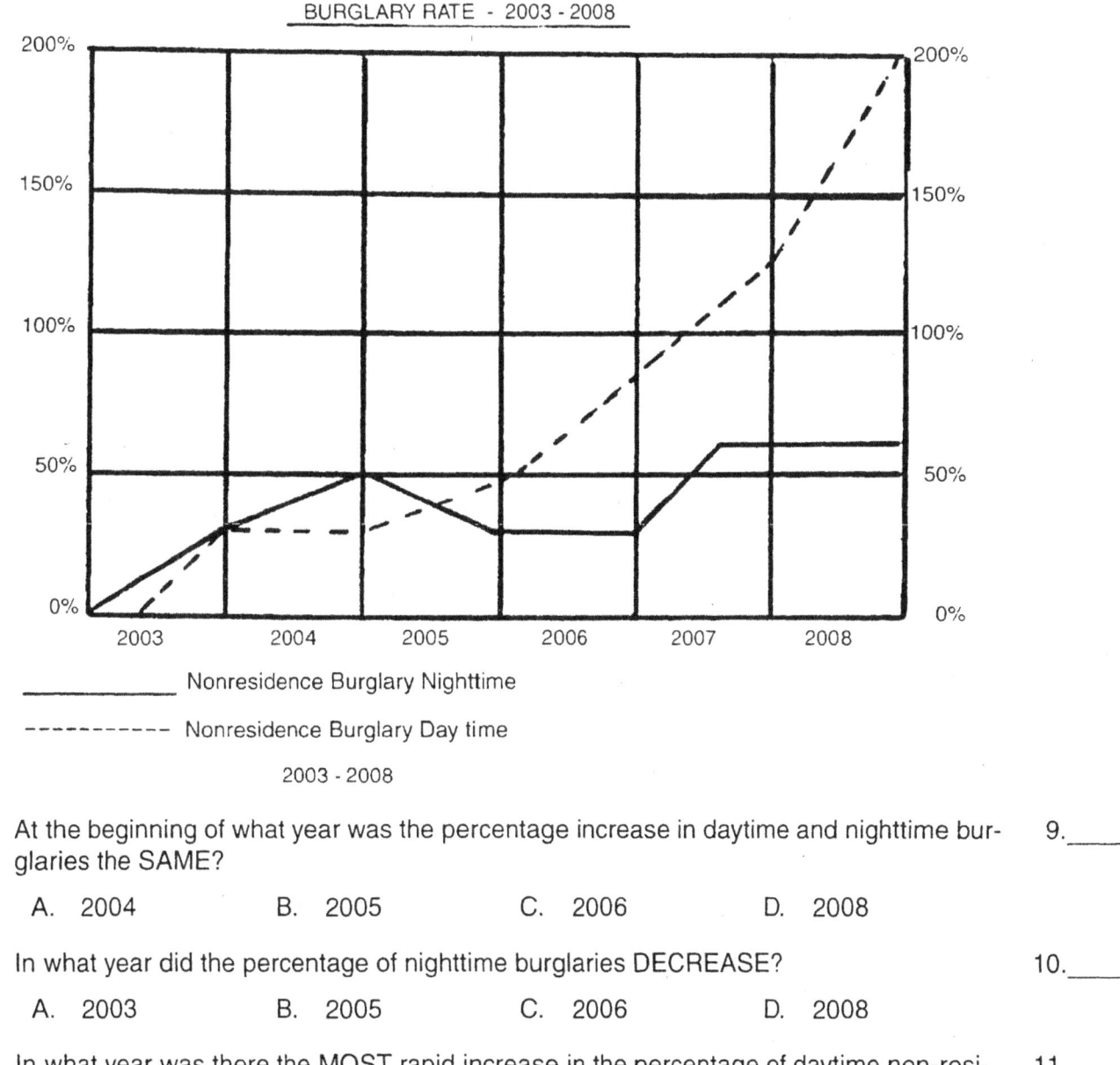

9. At the beginning of what year was the percentage increase in daytime and nighttime burglaries the SAME? 9._____

    A. 2004   B. 2005   C. 2006   D. 2008

10. In what year did the percentage of nighttime burglaries DECREASE? 10._____

    A. 2003   B. 2005   C. 2006   D. 2008

11. In what year was there the MOST rapid increase in the percentage of daytime non-residence burglaries? 11._____

    A. 2004   B. 2006   C. 2007   D. 2008

12. At the end of 2007, the actual number of nighttime burglaries committed 12._____

    A. was about 20%
    B. was 40%
    C. was 400
    D. cannot be determined from the information given

Questions 13-17.

DIRECTIONS: Questions 13 through 17 consist of two sentences numbered 1 and 2 taken from police officers' reports. Some of these sentences are correct according to ordinary formal English usage. Other sentences are incorrect because they contain errors in English usage or punctuation. Consider a sentence correct if it contains no errors in English usage or punctuation even if there may be other ways of writing the sentence correctly. Mark your answer to each question in the space at the right as follows:
A. If only sentence 1 is correct, but not sentence 2
B. If only sentence 2 is correct, but not sentence 1
C. If sentences 1 and 2 are both correct
D. If sentences 1 and 2 are both incorrect

SAMPLE QUESTION
1. The woman claimed that the purse was her's.
2. Everyone of the new officers was assigned to a patrol post.

EXPLANATION

Sentence 1 is INCORRECT because of an error in punctuation. The possessive words, "ours, yours, hers, theirs," do not have the apostrophe (').

Sentence 2 is CORRECT because the subject of the sentence is "Everyone" which is singular and requires the singular verb "was assigned".

Since only sentence 2 is correct, but not sentence 1, the CORRECT answer is B.

13. 1. Either the patrolman or his sergeant are always ready to help the public.   13._____
    2. The sergeant asked the patrolman when he would finish the report.

14. 1. The injured man could not hardly talk.   14._____
    2. Every officer had ought to hand in their reports on time.

15. 1. Approaching the victim of the assault, two large bruises were noticed by me.   15._____
    2. The prisoner was arrested for assault, resisting arrest, and use of a deadly weapon.

16. 1. A copy of the orders, which had been prepared by the captain, was given to each patrolman.   16._____
    2. It's always necessary to inform an arrested person of his constitutional rights before asking him any questions.

17. 1. To prevent further bleeding, I applied a tourniquet tothe wound.   17._____
    2. John Rano a senior officer was on duty at the time of the accident.

Questions 18-25.

DIRECTIONS: Answer each of Questions 18 through 25 SOLELY on the basis of the statement preceding the questions.

18. The criminal is one whose habits have been erroneously developed or, we should say, developed in anti-social patterns, and therefore the task of dealing with him is not one of punishment, but of treatment.   18._____
    The basic principle expressed in this statement is BEST illustrated by the

    A. emphasis upon rehabilitation in penal institutions
    B. prevalence of capital punishment for murder
    C. practice of imposing heavy fines for minor violations
    D. legal provision for trial by jury in criminal cases

19. The writ of habeas corpus is one of the great guarantees of personal liberty. Of the following, the BEST justification for this statement is that the writ of habeas corpus is frequently used to

    A. compel the appearance in court of witnesses who are outside the state
    B. obtain the production of books and records at a criminal trial
    C. secure the release of a person improperly held in custody
    D. prevent the use of deception in obtaining testimony of reluctant witnesses

    19._____

20. Fifteen persons suffered effects of carbon dioxide asphyxiation shortly before noon recently in a seventh-floor pressing shop. The accident occurred in a closed room where six steam presses were in operation. Four men and one woman were overcome.
    Of the following, the MOST probable reason for the fact that so many people were affected simultaneously is that

    A. women evidently show more resistance to the effects of carbon dioxide than men
    B. carbon dioxide is an odorless and colorless gas
    C. carbon dioxide is lighter than air
    D. carbon dioxide works more quickly at higher altitudes

    20._____

21. Lay the patient on his stomach, one arm extended directly overhead, the other arm bent at the elbow, and with the face turned outward and resting on hand or forearm.
    To the officer who is skilled at administering first aid, these instructions should IMMEDIATELY suggest

    A. application of artificial respiration
    B. treatment for third degree burns of the arm
    C. setting a dislocated shoulder
    D. control of capillary bleeding in the stomach

    21._____

22. The soda and acid fire extinguisher is the hand extinguisher most commonly used by officers. The main body of the cylinder is filled with a mixture of water and bicarbonate of soda. In a separate interior compartment, at the top, is a small bottle of sulphuric acid. When the extinguisher is inverted, the acid spills into the solution below and starts a chemical reaction. The carbon dioxide thereby generated forces the solution from the extinguisher.
    The officer who understands the operation of this fire extinguisher should know that it is LEAST likely to operate properly

    A. in basements or cellars
    B. in extremely cold weather
    C. when the reaction is of a chemical nature
    D. when the bicarbonate of soda is in solution

    22._____

23. Suppose that, at a training lecture, you are told that many of the men in our penal institutions today are second and third offenders.
    Of the following, the MOST valid inference you can make SOLELY on the basis of this statement is that

    A. second offenders are not easily apprehended
    B. patterns of human behavior are not easily changed
    C. modern laws are not sufficiently flexible
    D. laws do not breed crimes

    23._____

24. In all societies of our level of culture, acts are committed which arouse censure severe enough to take the form of punishment by the government. Such acts are crimes, not because of their inherent nature, but because of their ability to arouse resentment and to stimulate repressive measures.
Of the following, the MOST valid inference which can be drawn from this statement is that

    A. society unjustly punishes acts which are inherently criminal
    B. many acts are not crimes but are punished by society because such acts threaten the lives of innocent people
    C. only modern society has a level of culture
    D. societies sometimes disagree as to what acts are crimes

25. Crime cannot be measured directly. Its amount must be inferred from the frequency of some occurrence connected with it; for example, crimes brought to the attention of the police, persons arrested, prosecutions, convictions, and other dispositions, such as probation or commitment. Each of these may be used as an index of the amount of crime.
SOLELY on the basis of the foregoing statement, it is MOST correct to state that

    A. the incidence of crime cannot be estimated with any accuracy
    B. the number of commitments is usually greater than the number of probationary sentences
    C. the amount of crime is ordinarily directly correlated with the number of persons arrested
    D. a joint consideration of crimes brought to the attention of the police and the number of prosecutions undertaken gives little indication of the amount of crime in a locality

KEY (CORRECT ANSWERS)

1. B
2. A
3. D
4. C
5. D

6. B
7. A
8. A
9. A
10. B

11. D
12. D
13. D
14. D
15. B

16. C
17. A
18. A
19. C
20. B

21. A
22. B
23. B
24. D
25. C

EXAMINATION SECTION

TEST 1

DIRECTIONS: Each question or incomplete statement is followed by several suggested answers or completions. Select the one that BEST answers the question or completes the statement. *PRINT THE LETTER OF THE CORRECT ANSWER IN THE SPACE AT THE RIGHT.*

1. Upon arriving at the scene of an accident in which a pedestrian was struck and killed by an automobile, an officer's first action was to clear the scene of spectators.
   Of the following, the PRINCIPAL reason for this action is that
   A. important evidence may be inadvertently destroyed by the crowd
   B. this is a fundamental procedure in first aid work
   C. the operator of the vehicle may escape in the crowd
   D. witnesses will speak more freely if other persons are not present

   1.____

2. In questioning witnesses, an officer is instructed to avoid leading questions or questions that will suggest the answer.
   Accordingly, when questioning a witness about the appearance of a suspect, it would be BEST for him to ask:
   A. What kind of hat did he wear?   B. Did he wear a felt hat?
   C. What did he wear?   D. Didn't he wear a hat?

   2.____

3. The only personal description the police have of a particular criminal was made several years ago.
   Of the following, the item in the description that will be MOST useful in identifying him at the present time is the
   A. color of his eyes   B. color of his hair
   C. number of teeth   D. weight

   3.____

4. Crime statistics indicate that property crimes such as larceny, burglary, and robbery are more numerous during winter months than in summer.
   The one of the following explanations that MOST adequately accounts for this situation is that
   A. human needs, such as clothing, food, heat, and shelter, are greater in winter
   B. criminal tendencies are aggravated by climatic changes
   C. there are more hours of darkness in winter and such crimes are usually committed under cover of darkness
   D. urban areas are more densely populated during winter months, affording greater opportunity for such crimes

   4.____

5. When automobile tire tracks are to be used as evidence, a plaster cast is made of them.
   Of the following, the MOST probable reason for taking a photograph is that
   A. photographs can be duplicated more easily than castings
   B. less skill is required for photographing than casting
   C. the tracks may be damaged in the casting process
   D. photographs are more easily transported than castings

6. It is generally recommended that an officer, in lifting a revolver that is to be sent to the police laboratory for ballistics tests and fingerprint examination, do so by insetting a pencil through the trigger guard rather than into the barrel of the weapon.
   The reason for preferring this procedure is that
   A. every precaution must be taken not to eliminate fingerprints on the weapon
   B. there is a danger of accidentally discharging the weapon by placing the pencil in the barrel
   C. the pencil may make scratches inside the barrel that will interfere with the ballistics tests
   D. a weapon can more easily be lifted by the trigger guard

7. PHYSICIAN is to PATIENT as ATTORNEY is to
   A. court   B. client   C. counsel   D. judge

8. JUDGE is to SENTENCE as JURY is to
   A. court   B. foreman   C. defendant   D. verdict

9. REVERSAL is to AFFIRMANCE as CONVICTION is to
   A. appeal   B. acquittal   C. error   D. mistrial

10. GENUINE is to TRUE as SPURIOUS is to
    A. correct   B. conceived   C. false   D. speculative

11. ALLEGIANCE is to LOYALTY as TREASON is to
    A. felony   B. faithful   C. obedience   D. rebellion

12. CONCUR is to AGREE as DIFFER is to
    A. coincide   B. dispute   C. join   D. repeal

13. A person who has an uncontrollable desire to steal without need is called a
    A. dipsomaniac   B. kleptomaniac
    C. monomaniac   D. pyromaniac

14. In the sentence, "The placing of any inflammable substance in any building or the placing of any device or contrivence capable of producing fire, for the purpose of causing a fire is an attempt to burn," the MISSPELLED word is
    A. inflammable   B. substance   C. device   D. contrivence

15. In the sentence, "The word 'break' also means obtaining an entrance into a building by any artifice used for that purpose, or by colussion with any person therein," the MISSPELLED word is
    A. obtaining   B. entrance   C. artifice   D. colussion

16. In the sentence, "Any person who with intent to provoke a breech of the peace causes a disturbance or is offensive to others may be deemed to have committed disorderly conduct," the MISSPELLED word is
    A. breech   B. disturbance   C. offensive   D. committed

17. In the sentence, "When the offender inflicts a grevious harm upon the person from whose possession, or in his presence, property is taken, he is guilty of robbery, the MISSPELLED word is
    A. offender   B. grevious   C. possession   D. presence

18. In the sentence, "A person who wilfully encourages or advises another person in attempting to take the latter's life is guilty of a felony," the MISSPELLED word is
    A. wilfully   B. encourages   C. advises   D. attempting

19. The treatment to be given the offender cannot alter the fact of his offense; but we can take measures to reduce the chances of similar acts in the future. We should banish the criminal, not in order to exact revenge nor directly to encourage reform, but to deter him and others from further illegal attacks on society.
    According to this paragraph, the PRINCIPAL reason for punishing criminals is to
    A. prevent the commission of future crimes
    B. remove them safely from society
    C. avenge society
    D. teach them that crime does not pay

20. Even the most comprehensive and best substantiated summaries of the total volume of criminal acts would not contribute greatly to an understanding of the varied social and biological factors which are sometimes assumed to enter into crime causation, nor would they indicate with any degree of precision the needs of police forces in combating crime.
    According to this statement,
    A. crime statistics alone do not determine the needs of police forces in combating crime
    B. crime statistics are essential to a proper understanding of the social factors of crime
    C. social and biological factor which enter the crime causation have little bearing on police needs
    D. a knowledge of the social and biological factors of crime is essential to a proper understanding of crime statistics

4 (#1)

21. The police officer's art consists in applying and enforcing a multitude of laws and ordinances in such degree or proportion and in such manner that the greatest degree of social protection will be secured. The degree of enforcement and the method of application will vary with each neighborhood and community.
According to the foregoing paragraph,
   A. each neighborhood or community must judge for itself to what extent the law is to be enforced
   B. a police officer should only enforce those laws which are designed to give the greatest degree of social protection
   C. the manner and intensity of law enforcement is not necessarily the same in all communities
   D. all laws and ordinances must be enforced in a community with the same degree of intensity

21._____

22. Police control in the sense of regulating the details of police operations involves such matters as the technical means for so organizing the available personnel that competent police leadership, when secured, can operate effectively. It is concerned not so much with the extent to which popular controls can be trusted to guide and direct the course of police protection a with the administrative relationships which should exist between the component parts of the police organism.
According to the foregoing statement, police control is
   A. solely a matter of proper personnel assignment
   B. the means employed to guide and direct the course of police protection
   C. principally concerned with the administrative relationships between units of a police organization
   D. the sum total of means employed in rendering police protection

22._____

23. Two patrol cars hurry to the scene of an accident from different directions. The first proceeds at the rate of 45 miles per hour and arrives in four minutes. Although the second car travels over a route which is three-fourths of a mile longer, it arrives at the scene only a half-minute later.
The speed of the second car, expressed in miles per hour, is
   A. 50   B. 55   C. 60   D. 65

23._____

24. A motorcycle officer issued 72 traffic summonses in January, 60 in February and 83 in March.
In order to average 75 summonses per month for the four months of January, February, March, and April, during April he will have to issue _____ summonses.
   A. 80   B. 85   C. 90   D. 95

24._____

25. In a unit of the Police Department to which 40 officers are assigned, the sick report record during 2022 was as follows: 1 was absent 8 days, 5 were absent 3 days each, 4 were absent 5 days each, 10 were absent 2 days each, 8 were absent 4 days each, 5 were absent 1 day each.
The average number of days on sick report for all the members of this unit is MOST NEARLY
   A. ½   B. 1   C. 2 ½   D. 3

25._____

Questions 26-30.

DIRECTIONS: Column I lists various statements of fact. Column II is a list of crimes. Next to the numbers corresponding to the number preceding the statements of fact in Column I, place the letter preceding the crime listed in Column II with which Jones should be charged. In answering these questions, the following definitions of crimes should be applied, bearing in mind that ALL elements contained in the definitions must be present in order to charge a person with that crime.

BURGLARY is breaking and entering a building with intent to commit some crime therein. EMBEZZLEMENT is the appropriation to one's use of another's property which has been entrusted to one's care or which has come lawfully into one's possession. EXTORTION is taking or obtaining property from another with his consent, induced by a wrongful use of force or fear. LARCENY is taking and carrying away the personal property of another with intent to deprive or defraud the true owner of the use and benefit of such property. ROBBERY is the unlawful taking of the personal property of another from his person or in his presence by force or violence, or fear of injury.

COLUMN I

26. Jones, believing Smith had induced his wife to leave him, went to Smith's home armed with a knife with which he intended to assault Smith. When his knock was unanswered, he forced open the door of Smith's home and entered but, finding the house empty, he threw away the knife and left.

27. Jones was employed as a collection agent by Smith. When Smith refused to reimburse him for certain expenses he claimed to have incurred in connection with his work, Jones deducted this amount from sums he had collected for Smith.

28. Jones spent the night in a hotel. During the night he left his room, went downstairs to the desk, stole money and returned to his room.

29. Jones, a building inspector, found that the elevators in Smith's building were being operated without a permit. He threatened to report the matter and have the elevators shut down unless Smith paid him a sum of money. Smith paid the amount demanded

30. Jones held-up Smith on the street and, pointing a revolve at him, demanded his money. Smith, without resisting, handed Jones his money. When Jones was apprehended, it was discovered that the revolver was a toy.

COLUMN II

A. burglary
B. embezzlement
C. extortion
D. larceny
E. robbery
F. no crime

Questions 31-40.

DIRECTIONS: Questions 31 through 40 consist of statements from which a term is missing. Each of these statements can be completed correctly with one of the terms in the following list. In the space opposite the number corresponding to the number of the question, place the LETTER preceding the term in the following list which MOST accurately completes the statement.

A. affidavit	B. appeal	C. arraignment
D. arrest	E. bench warrant	F. habeas corpus
G. indictment	H. injunction	I. sentence
J. subpoena		

31. A _____ is a writ calling witnesses to court. 31._____

32. _____ is a method used to obtain a review of a case in court of superior jurisdiction. 32._____

33. A judgment passed by a court on a person on trial as a criminal offender is called a _____. 33._____

34. _____ is a writ or order requiring a person to refrain from a particular act. 34._____

35. _____ is the name given to a writ commanding the bringing of the body of a certain person before a certain court. 35._____

36. A _____ is a court order directing that an offender be brought into court. 36._____

37. The calling of a defendant before the court to answer an accusation is called _____. 37._____

38. The accusation in writing, presented by the grand jury to a competent court charging a person with a public offense is an _____. 38._____

39. A sworn declaration in writing is an _____. 39._____

40. _____ is the taking of a person into custody for the purpose of holding him to answer a criminal charge. 40._____

Questions 41-55.

DIRECTIONS: Questions 41 through 55 consist of statements from which a term is missing. Each of these statements can be completed correctly with one of the terms in the following list. In the space opposite the number corresponding to the number of the question, place the LETTER preceding the term in the following list which MOST accurately completes the statement.

A. accessory B. accomplice C. alibi
D. autopsy E. ballistics F. capital
G. confidence man H. commission I. conspiracy
J. corroborated K. grand jury L. homicide
M. misdemeanors N. penology O. perjury

41. _____ is the dissection of a dead human body to determine the cause of death. 41._____

42. The general term which mean the killing of one person by another is _____. 42._____

43. _____ is the science of the punishment of crime. 43._____

44. False swearing constitutes the crime of _____. 44._____

45. A combination of two or more persons to accomplish a criminal or unlawful act is called _____. 45._____

46. By _____ is meant evidence showing that a defendant was in another place when the crime was committed. 46._____

47. _____ is a term frequently used to describe a person engaged in a kind of swindling operation. 47._____

48. A _____ offense is one for which a life sentence or death penalty is prescribed by law. 48._____

49. A violation of a law may be either an act of omission or an act of _____. 49._____

50. An _____ is a person who is liable to prosecution for the identical offense charged against a defendant on trial. 50._____

51. A person would be an _____ who after the commission of a crime aided in the escape of one he knew to be an offender. 51._____

52. An official body called to hear complaints and to determine whether there is ground for criminal prosecution is known as the _____. 52._____

53. Crimes are generally divided into two classes, namely felonies and _____. 53._____

54. _____ is the science of the motion of projectiles. 54._____

55. Testimony of a witness which is confirmed by another witness is _____. 55._____

Questions 56-60.

DIRECTIONS: Next to the question number which corresponds with the number of each item in Column I, place the letter preceding the adjective in Column II which BEST describes the persons in Column I.

COLUMN I	COLUMN II	
56. A talkative woman	A. abstemious	56.____
57. A person on a reducing diet	B. pompous C. erudite	57.____
58. A scholarly professor	D. benevolent E. docile	58.____
59. A man who seldom speaks	F. loquacious G. indefatigable	59.____
60. A charitable person	H. taciturn	60.____

Questions 61-65.

DIRECTIONS: Next to the question number which corresponds with the number preceding each profession in Column I, place the letter preceding the word in Column II which BEST explains the subject of that profession.

COLUMN I	COLUMN II	
61. Geologist	A. animals	61.____
62. Oculist	B. eyes C. feet	62.____
63. Podiatrist	D. fortune-telling E. language	63.____
64. Palmist	F. rocks G. stamps	64.____
65. Zoologist	H. woman	65.____

Questions 66-70.

DIRECTIONS: Next to the question number corresponding to the number of each of the words in Column I, place the letter preceding the word in Column II that is MOST NEARLY OPPOSITE to it in meaning.

COLUMN I	COLUMN II	
66. comely	A. beautiful	66.____
67. eminent	B. cowardly C. kind	67.____
68. frugal	D. sedate E. shrewd	68.____
69. gullible	F. ugly G. unknown	69.____
70. valiant	H. wasteful	70.____

KEY (CORRECT ANSWERS)

1. A	16. A	31. J	46. C	61. F
2. C	17. B	32. B	47. G	62. B
3. A	18. A	33. I	48. F	63. C
4. C	19. A	34. H	49. H	64. D
5. C	20. A	35. F	50. B	65. A
6. C	21. C	36. E	51. A	66. F
7. B	22. C	37. C	52. L	67. G
8. D	23. A	38. G	53. N	68. H
9. B	24. B	39. A	54. E	69. E
10. C	25. C	40. D	55. K	70. B
11. D	26. A	41. D	56. F	
12. B	27. B	42. M	57. A	
13. B	28. D	43. O	58. C	
14. D	29. C	44. P	59. H	
15. D	30. E	45. J	60. D	

EXAMINATION SECTION
TEST 1

DIRECTIONS: Each question or incomplete statement is followed by several suggested answers or completions. Select the one that BEST answers the question or completes the statement. *PRINT THE LETTER OF THE CORRECT ANSWER IN THE SPACE AT THE RIGHT.*

1. The delivery of an arrested person to his sureties, upon their giving security for his appearance at the time and place designated to submit to the jurisdiction and judgment of the court, is known as
   A. bail
   B. habeas corpus
   C. parole
   D. probation

1.____

2. Jones was charged with the murder of Smith. Brown, Jones' landlord, testified at the trial that Jones had in his home a well-equipped laboratory which contained all the necessary chemical for producing the poison which an autopsy showed caused Smith's death.
   Brown's testimony constitutes what is called _____ evidence.
   A. corroborative   B. opinion   C. hearsay   D. circumstantial

2.____

3. In addressing a class of recruits, a police lieutenant remarked: "Carelessness and failure are twins."
   The one of the following that MOST NEARLY expresses his meaning is
   A. negligence seldom accompanies success
   B. incomplete work is careless work
   C. conscientious work is never attended by failure
   D. a conscientious person never makes mistakes

3.____

4. In taking a statement from a person who has been shot by an assailant and is not expected to live, police are instructed to ask the person: "Do you believe you are about to die?"
   Of the following, the MOST probable reason for this question is
   A. the theory that a person about to die will tell the truth
   B. to determine if the victim is conscious and capable of making a statement
   C. to put the victim mentally at ease and more willing to talk
   D. that the statement could not be used in court if his mind was distraught by the fear of impending death

4.____

5. If, while you are on duty at a busy intersection, a pedestrian asks you for directions to a particular place, the BEST course of conduct is to
   A. ignore the question and continue directing operations
   B. tell the pedestrian to ask a patrolman on foot patrol
   C. answer the question in a brief, courteous manner
   D. leave your post only long enough to give clear and adequate directions

5.____

6. In lecturing on the law of arrest, a lieutenant remarked: "To go beyond is as bad as to fall short."
The one of the following which MOST NEARLY expresses his meaning is
   A. never undertake the impossible   B. extremes are not desirable
   C. look before you leap   D. too much success is dangerous

7. Suppose you are an officer assigned to a patrol precinct. While you are in the vicinity of a school, your attention is called to a man who is selling small packages to school children. You are told that this man distributes similar packages to these same children daily and that he is suspected of dealing in narcotics.
Of the following, the BEST action for you to take is to
   A. pretend to be an addict and attempt to purchase narcotics from him
   B. observe the man's action yourself for several days in order to obtain grounds for arrest
   C. stop and question one or more of the children after they have transacted business with the man
   D. stop and question the man as he leaves the children

8. In the event of a poison gas attack, civil defense authorities advise civilians to _____ door and windows and go to _____.
   A. open; upper floors   B. close; upper floors
   C. open; the basement   D. close; the basement

9. The procedure whereby a defendant is brought before a magistrate, informed of the charge against him, and asked how he pleads thereto, is called
   A. arraignment   B. indictment   C. presentment   D. inquisition

10. A written accusation of a crime presented by a grand jury is called a(n)
    A. commitment   B. arraignment   C. indictment   D. demurrer

11. The one of the following statements made by a prisoner that is correctly called an alibi is:
    A. "He struck me first."
    B. "I didn't intend to hurt him."
    C. "I was miles away from there at the time."
    D. "I don't remember what happened."

12. A person who, after the commission of a crime, conceals the defender with the intent that the latter may escape from arrest and trial, is called a(n)
    A. accessory   B. accomplice   C. confederate   D. associate

13. A sworn statement of fact is called a(n)
    A. affidavit   B. oath
    C. acknowledgment   D. subpoena

14. The right of trial by jury in the courts of the state is PRIMARILY safeguarded by a provision of
    A. the United States Constitution
    B. the constitution of the state
    C. a state statute
    D. a Federal statute

15. The task of protecting the President and his family is entrusted PRIMARILY to the
    A. Federal Bureau of Investigation
    B. United States Secret Service
    C. Central Intelligence Agency
    D. District of Columbia Police Department

16. The coordinating organization for the various Federal agencies engaged in intelligence activities is the
    A. Federal Bureau of Investigation
    B. Federal Security Agency
    C. Mutual Security Agency
    D. Central Intelligence Agency

17. A drug addict whose arm shows many scars from the injection of a hypodermic needle is MOST apt to be addicted to
    A. heroin   B. cocaine   C. opium   D. marijuana

18. All of the following drugs are derived from opium EXCEPT
    A. cocaine   B. heroin   C. morphine   D. codeine

19. In addition to cases of submersion, artificial respiration is a recommended first aid procedure for
    A. sunstroke
    B. chemical poisoning
    C. electric shock
    D. apoplexy

20. An injury to a muscle or tendon brought about by severe exertion and resulting in pain and stiffness is called a
    A. strain   B. sprain   C. bruise   D. fracture

21. Of the following kinds of wounds, the one in which there is the LEAST danger of infection is a(n) _____ wound.
    A. abrasive   B. punctured   C. lacerated   D. incised

22. When a person is found injured on the street, it is generally advisable, pending arrival of a physician, to help prevent fainting or shock by keeping the patient
    A. in a sitting position
    B. lying down with the head level
    C. lying down with the head raised
    D. standing on his feet

23. When an injured person appears to be suffering from shock, of the following, it is MOST essential to
    A. loosen his clothing
    B. keep him warm
    C. administer a stimulant
    D. place him in a prone position

24. In the sentence, "Malice was immanent in all his remarks," the word "immanent" means MOST NEARLY
    A. elevated   B. inherent   C. threatening   D. foreign

25. In the sentence, "The extant copies of the document were found in the safe," the word "extant" means MOST NEARLY
    A. existing   B. original   C. forged   D. duplicate

26. In the sentence, "The recruit was more complaisant after the captain spoke to him," the word "complaisant" means MOST NEARLY
    A. calm   B. affable   C. irritable   D. confident

27. In the sentence, "The man was captured under highly creditable circumstances," the word "creditable" means MOST NEARLY
    A. doubtful   B. believable   C. praiseworthy   D. unexpected

28. In the sentence, "His superior officers were more sagacious than he," the word "sagacious" means MOST NEARLY
    A. shrewd   B. obtuse   C. absurd   D. verbose

29. In the sentence, "He spoke with impunity," the word "impunity" means MOST NEARLY
    A. rashness   B. caution   C. without fear   D. immunity

30. In the sentence, "The new patrolman displayed unusual temerity during the emergency," the word "temerity" means MOST NEARLY
    A. fear   B. rashness   C. calmness   D. anxiety

31. In the sentence, "The portions of food were parsimoniously served," the word "parsimoniously means MOST NEARLY
    A. stingily   B. piously   C. elaborately   D. generously

32. In the sentence, "Generally the speaker's remarks were sententious," the word "sententious means MOST NEARLY
    A. verbose
    B. witty
    C. argumentative
    D. pithy

33. In the sentence, "The prisoner was fractious when brought to the station house," the word "fractious" means MOST NEARLY
    A. penitent   B. talkative   C. irascible   D. broken-hearted

34. In the sentence, "The judge was implacable when the attorney pleaded for leniency," the word "implacable" means MOST NEARLY
    A. inexorable
    B. disinterested
    C. inattentive
    D. indifferent

35. In the sentence, "The court ordered the mendacious statements stricken from the record," the word "mendacious" means MOST NEARLY
    A. begging   B. lying   C. threatening   D. lengthy

36. In the sentence, "The district attorney spoke in a strident voice," the word "strident" means MOST NEARLY
    A. loud
    B. harsh-sounding
    C. sing-song
    D. low

37. In the sentence, "The speaker had a predilection for long sentences," the word "predilection" means MOST NEARLY
    A. aversion   B. talent   C. propensity   D. diffidence

38. In the sentence, "The candidate wants to file his application for preference before it is too late," the word "before" is used as a(n)
    A. preposition
    B. subordinating conjunction
    C. pronoun
    D. adverb

39. The one of the following sentences which is grammatically PREFERABLE to the others is:
    A. Our engineers will go over your blueprints so that you may have no problems in construction.
    B. For a long time he had been arguing that we, not he, are to blame for the confusion.
    C. I worked on this automobile for two hours and still cannot find out what is wrong with it.
    D. Accustomed to all kinds of hardships, fatigue seldom bothers veteran policemen.

40. The plural of
    A. turkey is turkies
    B. cargo is cargoes
    C. bankruptcy is bankruptcys
    D. son-in-law is son-in-laws

41. The abbreviation "viz." means MOST NEARLY
    A. namely   B. for example   C. the following   D. see

42. In the sentence, "A man in a light-grey suit waited thirty-five minutes in the ante-room for the all-important document," the word IMPROPERLY hyphenated is
    A. light-grey   B. thirty-five   C. ante-room   D. all-important

43. The MOST accurate of the following sentences is:
    A. The commissioner, as well as his deputy and various bureau heads, were present.
    B. A new organization of employers and employees have been formed.
    C. One or the other of these men have been selected.
    D. The number of pages in the book is enough to discourage a reader.

44. The MOST accurate of the following sentences is:
    A. Between you and me, I think he is the better man.
    B. He was believed to be me.
    C. Is it us that you wish to see?
    D. The winners are him and her.

45. In the sentence, "The committee favored submiting the amendment to the electorate," the MISSPELLED word is
    A. committee   B. submiting   C. amendment   D. electorate

46. In the sentence, "He maliciously demurred to an ajournment of the proceedings," the MISSPELLED word is
    A. maliciously   B. demurred   C. ajournment   D. proceedings

47. In the sentence, "His innocence at that time is irrelevent in view of his more recent villainous demeanor," the MISSPELLED word is
    A. innocence   B. irrelevent   C. villainous   D. demeanor

48. In the sentence, "The mischievous boys aggrevated the annoyance of their neighbor," the MISSPELLED word is
    A. mischievous   B. aggrevated   C. annoyance   D. neighbor

49. In the sentence, "While his persiverance was commendable, his judgment was debatable, the MISSPELLED word is
    A. persiverance   B. commendable
    C. judgment   D. debatable

50. In the sentence, "He was hoping the appeal would facilitate his aquittal," the MISSPELLED word is
    A. hoping   B. appeal   C. facilitate   D. aquittal

51. In the sentence, "It would be preferable for them to persue separate courses," the MISSPELLED word is
    A. preferable   B. persue   C. separate   D. courses

52. In the sentence, "The litigant was complimented on his persistance and achievement," the MISSPELLED word is
    A. litigant   B. complimented
    C. persistance   D. achievement

53. In the sentence, "Ocassionally there are discrepancies in the descriptions of miscellaneous items," the MISSPELLED word is
    A. ocassionally   B. discrepancies
    C. descriptions   D. miscellaneous

54. In the sentence, "The councilmanic seargent-at-arms enforced the prohibition," the MISSPELLED word is
    A. councilmanic   B. seargent-at-arms
    C. enforced   D. prohibition

55. In the sentence, "The teacher had an ingenious device for mantaining attendance," the MISSPELLED word is
    A. ingenious   B. device   C. mantaining   D. attendance

Questions 56-63.

DIRECTIONS: Questions 56 through 63 are to be answered on the basis of the following excerpt from a recorded annual report of the police department. This material should be read first and then referred to in answering these questions, which are to be answered SOLELY on the basis of the material herein contained.

LEGAL BUREAU

One of the more important functions of this bureau is to analyze and furnish the department with pertinent information concerning Federal and State statutes and Local Laws which affect the department, law enforcement or crime prevention. In addition, all measures introduced in the State Legislature and the City Council which may affect this department are carefully reviewed by members of the Legal Bureau and, where necessary, opinions and recommendations thereon are prepared.

Another important function of this office is the prosecution of cases in the Magistrate's Courts. This is accomplished by assignment of attorneys who are members of the Legal Bureau to appear in those cases which are deemed to raise issues of importance to the department or questions of law which require technical presentation to facilitate proper determination; and also in those cases where request is made for such appearances by a magistrate, some other official of the city, or a member of the force. Attorneys are regularly assigned to prosecute all cases in the Women's Court.

Proposed legislation was prepared and sponsored for introduction in the State Legislature and, at this writing, one of these proposals has already been enacted into law and five others are presently on the Governor's desk awaiting executive action. The new law prohibits the sale or possession of a hypodermic syringe or needle by an unauthorized person. The bureau's proposals awaiting executive action pertain to an amendment to the Code of Criminal Procedure prohibiting desk officers from taking bail in gambling cases or in cases mentioned in Section 552, Code of Criminal Procedure; including confidence men and swindlers as jostlers in the Penal Law; prohibiting the sale of switchblade knives of any size to children under 16 and bills extending the licensing period of gunsmiths.

The Legal Bureau has regularly cooperated with the Corporation Counsel and the District Attorneys in respect to matters affecting this department, and has continued to advise and represent the Police Athletic League, the Police Sports Association, the Police Relief Fund, and the Police Pension Fund.

The following is a statistical report of the activities of the bureau during the current year as compared with the previous year:

	Current Year	Previous Year
Memoranda of law prepared	68	83
Legal matters forwarded to corporation counsel	122	144
Letters requesting legal information	756	807
Letters requesting departmental records	139	111
Matters for publication	17	26
Court appearances of members of bureau	4,678	4,621
Conferences	94	103
Lectures at Police Academy	30	33
Reports on proposed legislation	194	255
Deciphering of codes	79	27
Expert testimony	31	16
Notices to court witnesses	55	81
Briefs prepared	22	18
Court papers prepared	258	--

56. One of the functions of the Legal Bureau is to
    A. review and make recommendations on proposed Federal laws affecting law enforcement
    B. prepare opinions on all measures introduced in the State Legislature and the City Council
    C. furnish the Police Department with pertinent information concerning all new Federal and State laws
    D. analyze all laws affecting the work of the Police Department

57. The one of the following that is NOT a function of the Legal Bureau is
    A. law enforcement and crime prevention
    B. prosecution of all cases in Women's Court
    C. advise and represent the Police Sports Association
    D. lecturing at the Police Academy

58. Members of the Legal Bureau frequently appear in Magistrate's Court for the purpose of
    A. defending members of the Police Force
    B. raising issues of importance to the Police Department
    C. prosecuting all offenders arrested by members of the Force
    D. facilitating proper determination of questions of law requiring technical presentation

59. The Legal Bureau sponsored a bill that would
    A. extend the licenses of gunsmiths
    B. prohibit the sale of switchblade knives to children of any size
    C. place confidence men and swindlers in the same category as jostlers in the Penal Law
    D. prohibit desk officers from admitting gamblers, confidence men, and swindlers to bail

60. From the report, it is NOT reasonable to infer that
    A. fewer bills affecting the Police Department were introduced in the current year
    B. the preparation of court papers was a new activity assumed in the current year
    C. the Code of Criminal Procedure authorizes desk officers to accept bail in certain cases
    D. the penalty for jostling and swindling is the same

61. According to the statistical report, the activity showing the GREATEST percentage of decrease in the current year as compared to the previous year was
    A. matters for publication
    B. reports on proposed legislation
    C. notices to court witnesses
    D. memoranda of law prepared

62. According to the statistical report, the activity showing the GREATEST percentage of increase in the current year as compare with the previous year was
    A. court appearances of members of the bureau
    B. giving expert testimony
    C. deciphering of codes
    D. letters requesting departmental records

63. According to the report, the percentage of bills prepared and sponsored by the Legal Bureau which were passed by the State Legislature and sent to the Governor for approval was APPROXIMATELY
    A. 3.1%
    B. 2.6%
    C. .5%
    D. not capable of determination from the data given

64. A squad of officers assigned to enforce a new parking regulation in a particular area issued tag summonses on a particular day as follows: four officers issued 16 summonses each; three issued 19 each; one issued 22; seven issued 25 each; eleven issued 28 each; ten issued 30 each; two issued 36 each; one issued 41; and three issued 45 each.
    The average number of summonses issued by a member of this squad was MOST NEARLY
    A. 6.2   B. 17.2   C. 21.0   D. 27.9

65. A water storage tank is 75 feet long and 30 feet wide and has a depth of 6½ feet. Each cubic foot of the tank holds 9½ gallons.
    The TOTAL capacity of the tank is _____ gallons.
    A. 73,125½   B. 131,625   C. 138,937½   D. 146,250

66. The price of admission to a PAL entertainment were $2.50 each for adults and $1.00 for children; the turnstile at the entrance showed that 358 persons entered and the gate receipts were $626.50.
The number of children who attended was
A. 170   B. 175   C. 179   D. 183

66._____

67. A patrol car travels six times as fast as a bicycle.
If the patrol car goes 168 miles in two hours less time than the bicycle requires to go 42 miles, their respective rates of speed are _____ miles per hour.
A. 36 and 6   B. 42 and 7   C. 63 and 10½   D. 126 and 21

67._____

68. The radiator of an automobile already contains six quarts of a 10% solution of alcohol.
In order to make a mixture of 20% alcohol, it will be necessary to add _____ quarts of alcohol.
A. ¾   B. 1¾   C. 2½   D. 3

68._____

69. A man received an inheritance of $80,000 and wanted to invest it so that it would produce an annual income sufficient to pay his rent of $400 a month.
In order to do this, he will have to receive interest or dividends at the rate of _____% per annum.
A. 3   B. 4   C. 5¾   D. 6

69._____

70. If the price of a bus ticket varies *directly* as the mileage involved, and a ticket to travel 135 miles costs $29.70, a ticket for a 30-mile trip will cost
A. $15.20   B. $13.40   C. $6.60   D. $2.20

70._____

71. A man owed a debt of $5,800. After a first payment of $100, he agreed to pay the balance by monthly payments in which each payment after this first would be $20 more than that of the preceding month.
If no interest charge is made, he will have to make, including the first payment, a total of _____ monthly payments.
A. 16   B. 20   C. 24   D. 28

71._____

72. The written test of a civil service examination has a weight of 30, the oral test a weight of 20, experience a weight of 20, and the physical test a weight of 30. A candidate received ratings of 76 on the written test, 84 on the oral, and 80 for experience.
In order to attain an average of 85 on the examination, his rating on the physical test must be
A. 86   B. 90   C. 94   D. 98

72._____

73. A family has an income of $3,200 per month. It spends 22% of this amount for rent, 36% for food, 16% for clothing, and 12% for additional household expenses. After meeting these expenses, 50% of the balance is deposited in the bank.
The amount deposited monthly is
A. $224.00   B. $366.00   C. $448.00   D. $520.00

73._____

74. Upon retirement last July, an officer bought a farm of 64 acres for $18,000 per acre. He made a down payment of $612,000 and agreed to pay the balance in installments of $7,500 a month commencing on August 1, 2022. Disregarding interest, he will make his LAST payment in
   A. July 2028
   B. August 2030
   C. January 2032
   D. April 2035

75. 40% of those who commit a particular crime are subsequently arrested and convicted. 75% of those committed receive sentences of 10 years or more. Assuming that those arrested for the first time serve less than 10 years, the percentage of those committing this crime who receive sentences of ten years or more is MOST NEARLY
   A. 20%
   B. 30%
   C. 40%
   D. 50%

KEY (CORRECT ANSWERS)

1.	A	21.	D	41.	A	61.	A
2.	D	22.	B	42.	C	62.	C
3.	A	23.	B	43.	D	63.	D
4.	A	24.	B	44.	A	64.	D
5.	C	25.	A	45.	B	65.	C
6.	B	26.	B	46.	C	66.	C
7.	C	27.	C	47.	C	67.	B
8.	B	28.	A	48.	B	68.	A
9.	A	29.	D	49.	A	69.	D
10.	C	30.	B	50.	D	70.	C
11.	C	31.	A	51.	B	71.	B
12.	A	32.	D	52.	C	72.	D
13.	A	33.	C	53.	A	73.	A
14.	B	34.	A	54.	B	74.	A
15.	B	35.	B	55.	C	75.	B
16.	D	36.	B	56.	D		
17.	A	37.	C	57.	A		
18.	A	38.	B	58.	D		
19.	C	39.	A	59.	C		
20.	A	40.	B	60.	D		

VISUAL RECALL

EXAMINATION SECTION
TEST 1

DIRECTIONS: Each question or incomplete statement is followed by several suggested answers or completions. Select the one that BEST answers the question or completes the statement. *PRINT THE LETTER OF THE CORRECT ANSWER IN THE SPACE AT THE RIGHT.* This test consists of four(4) pictures with questions following each picture. Study each picture for three (3) minutes. Then answer the questions based upon what you remember without looking back at the pictures.

Questions 1-5

DIRECTIONS: Questions 1 through 5 are based on the drawing below showing a view of a waiting area in a public building.

1. A desk is shown in the drawing. Which of the following is on the desk? 1._____
    A(n)

    A. plant   B. telephone
    C. in-out file   D. *Information* sign

2. On which floor is the waiting area? 2._____

    A. Basement   B. Main floor
    C. Second floor   D. Third floor

3. The door <u>immediately to the right</u> of the desk is a(n) 3._____

    A. door to the Personnel Office
    B. elevator door
    C. door to another corridor
    D. door to the stairs

4. Among the magazines on the tables in the waiting area are 4._____

    A. TIME and NEWSWEEK
    B. READER'S DIGEST and T.V. GUIDE
    C. NEW YORK and READER'S DIGEST
    D. TIME and T.V. GUIDE

5. One door is partly open. 5._____
    This is the door to

    A. the Director's office
    B. the Personnel Manager's office
    C. the stairs
    D. an unmarked office

Questions 6-9.

DIRECTIONS: Questions 6 through 9 are based on the drawing below showing the contents of a male suspect's pockets.

6. The suspect had a slip in his pockets showing an appointment at an out-patient clinic on   6.____

   A. February 9, 2009
   B. September 2, 2008
   C. February 19, 2008
   D. September 12, 2009

7. The transistor radio that was found on the suspect was made by   7.____

   A. RCA   B. GE   C. Sony   D. Zenith

8. The coins found in the suspect's pockets have a TOTAL value of   8.____

   A. 56¢   B. 77¢   C. $1.05   D. $1.26

9. All except one of the following were found in the suspect's pockets.   9.____
   Which was NOT found?
   A

   A. ticket stub   B. comb
   C. subway token   D. pen

Questions 10-13.

DIRECTIONS: Questions 10 through 13 are based on the picture showing the contents of a woman's handbag. Assume that all of the contents are shown in the picture.

4 (#1)

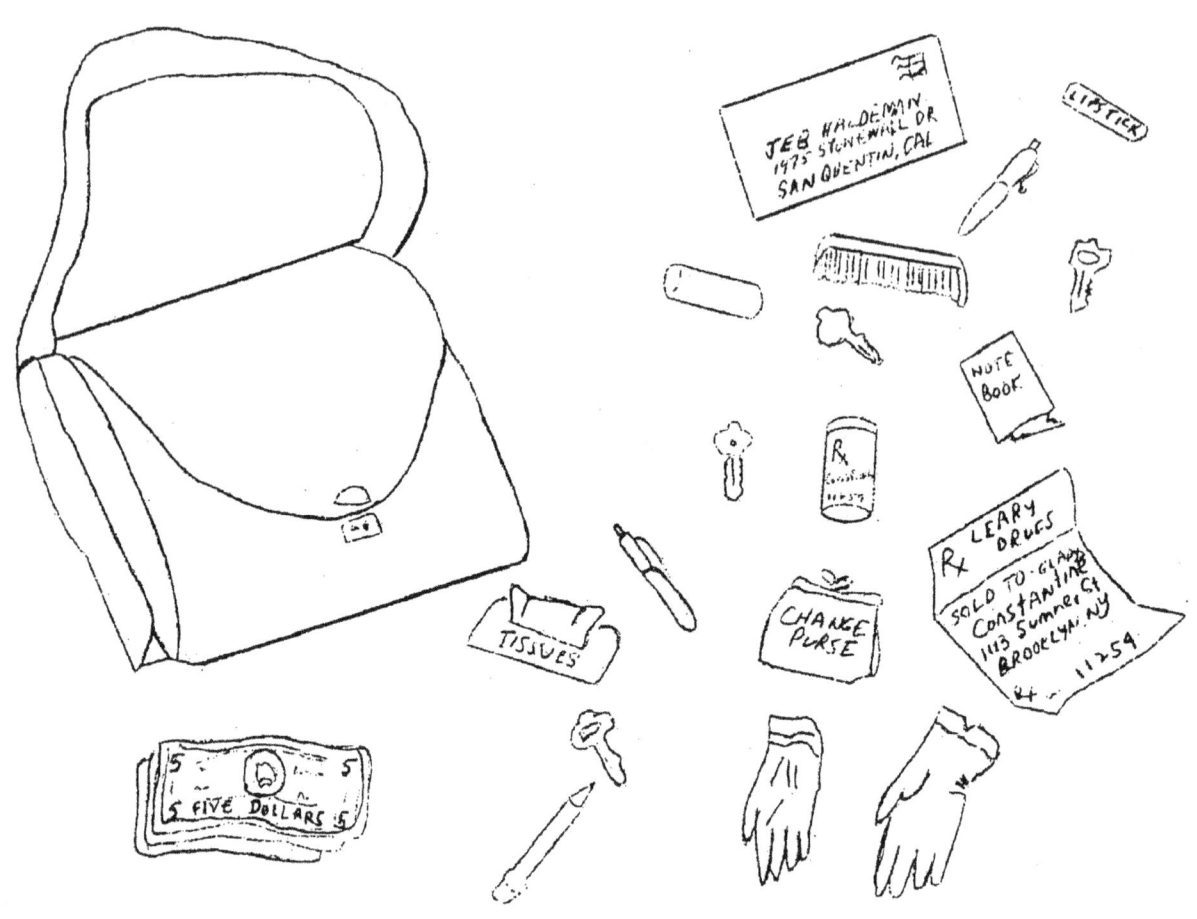

10. Where does Gladys Constantine live? 10.____
    _____ Street in _____.

    A. Chalmers; Manhattan   B. Summer; Manhattan
    C. Summer; Brooklyn   D. Chalmers; Brooklyn

11. How many keys were in the handbag? 11.____

    A. 2   B. 3   C. 4   D. 5

12. How much money was in the handbag? 12.____
    _____ dollar(s).

    A. Exactly five   B. More than five
    C. Exactly ten   D. Less than one

13. The sales slip found in the handbag shows the purchase of which of the following? 13.____

    A. The handbag   B. Lipstick
    C. Tissues   D. Prescription medicine

Questions 14-18.

DIRECTIONS: Questions 14 through 18 are based on the street scene on the following page. A robbery may be in progress down the block from where you are standing. Study and memorize the details before answering these questions.

14. The man carrying the two shopping bags is wearing   14._____

    A. khaki shorts and work boots
    B. a hat and black jacket
    C. a zip-up fleece and glasses
    D. a casual shirt and jeans

15. The building at the center of the photo is a(n)   15._____

    A. hotel   B. bank   C. restaurant   D. office building

16. The sidewalk is lined on the street side with   16._____

    A. parking meters   B. safety pillars
    C. street vendors   D. flower beds

17. Among the people standing in front of the center building is a   17._____

    A. man wearing khaki pants
    B. woman wearing knee-high boots
    C. young boy chasing another young boy
    D. man wearing a sports jersey

18. Reflections in the store windows indicate that 18.____

    A. there are food carts parked in the street
    B. a white truck is driving nearby
    C. it is a very sunny day
    D. a man is sitting on a curb nearby

KEY (CORRECT ANSWERS)

1.	D		11.	C
2.	C		12.	B
3.	B		13.	D
4.	D		14.	C
5.	B		15.	A
6.	A		16.	D
7.	C		17.	A
8.	D		18.	B
9.	D			
10.	C			

EXAMINATION SECTION

TEST 1

DIRECTIONS: Each question or incomplete statement is followed by several suggested answers or completions. Select the one that BEST answers the question or completes the statement. *PRINT THE LETTER OF THE CORRECT ANSWER IN THE SPACE AT THE RIGHT.*

Questions 1-4.

DIRECTIONS: Questions 1 through 4 measure your ability to recognize objects, people, events, parts of maps, or crime, accident, or other scenes to which you have been exposed.

Below and on the following pages are twenty illustrations. Study them carefully. In the test, you will be shown pairs of drawings. For each pair, you will be asked which is or are from the twenty illustrations in this part.

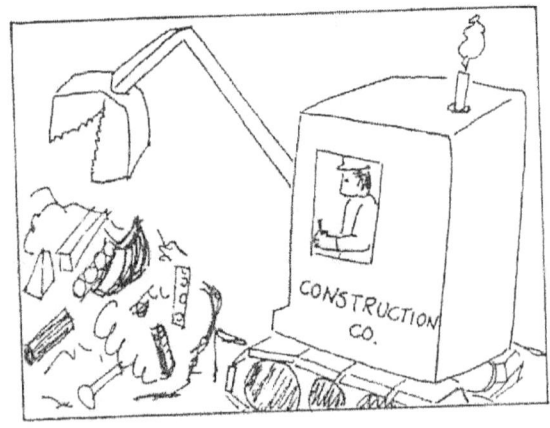
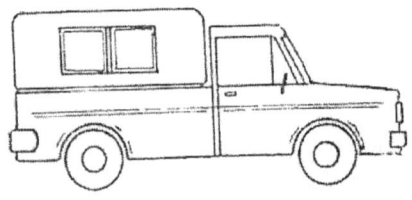

4 (#1)

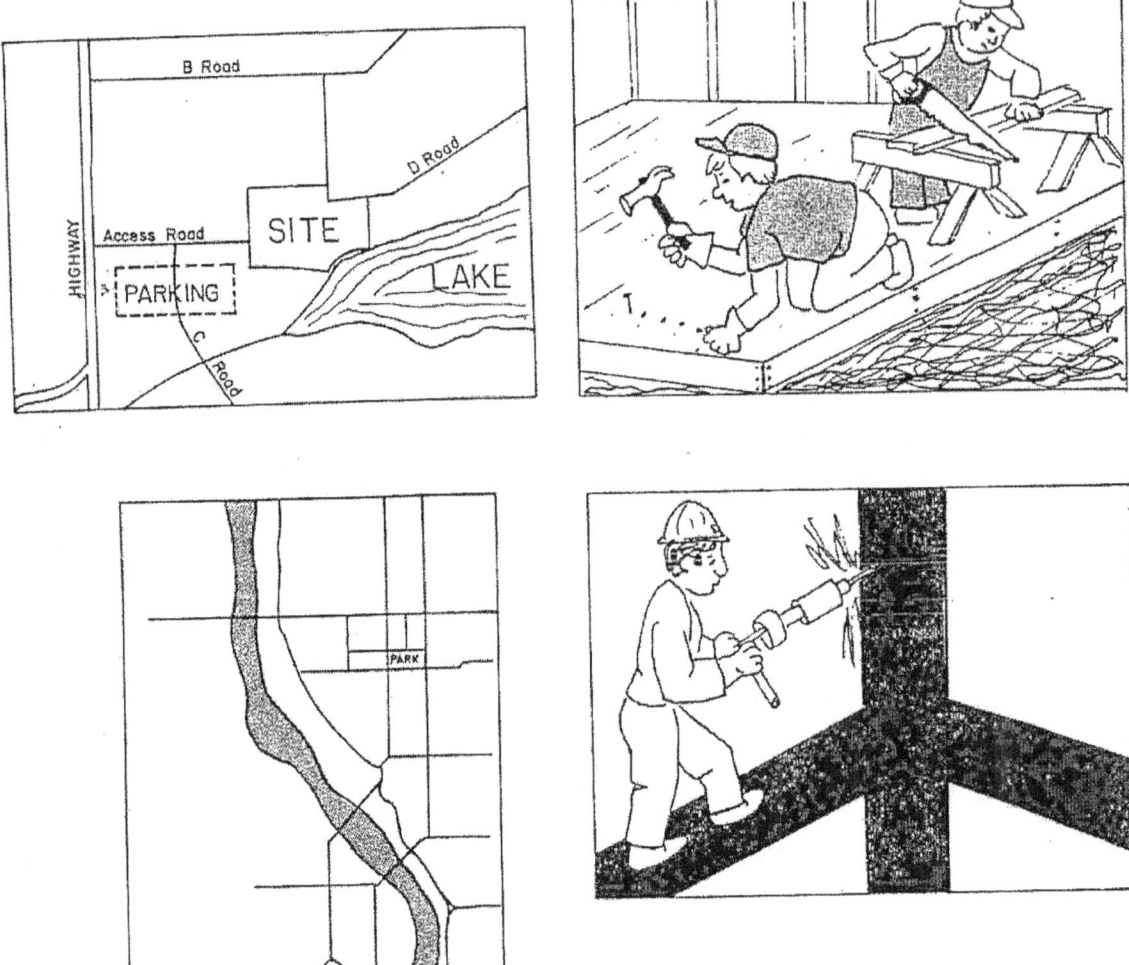

Questions 1-4.

DIRECTIONS: In Questions 1 through 4, select the choice that corresponds to the scene(s) that is(are) from the illustrations for this section. *PRINT THE LETTER OF THE CORRECT ANSWER IN THE SPACE AT THE RIGHT.*

1.
   I
   II

   A. I only
   B. II only
   C. Both I and II
   D. Neither I nor II

   2.____

2.
   I
   II

   A. I only
   B. II only
   C. Both I and II
   D. Neither I nor II

   2.____

3.

A. I only B. II only
C. Both I and II D. Neither I nor II

4.

A. I only B. II only
C. Both I and II D. Neither I nor II

Questions 5-6.

DIRECTIONS: Questions 5 and 6 measure your ability to notice and interpret details accurately. You will be shown a picture, below, and then asked a set of questions about the picture. You do NOT need to memorize this picture. You may look at the picture when answering the questions.

5.

Details in the picture lend some support to or do NOT tend to contradict which of the following statements about the person who occupies the room?
I. The person is very careless.
II. The person smokes.
The CORRECT answer is:
   A. I only
   B. II only
   C. Both I and II
   D. Neither I nor II

6. The number on the piece of paper on the desk is MOST likely a 6.____
   A. ZIP code
   B. street number
   C. social security number
   D. telephone area code

Questions 7-10.

DIRECTIONS: Questions 7 through 10 measure your ability to recognize objects or people in differing views, contexts, or situations. Each question consists of three pictures; one labeled I and one labeled II. In each question, you are to determine whether A – I only, B – II only, C – Both I and II, and D – Neither I nor II COULD be the subject.

The Subject is *always* ONE person or ONE object. The Subject picture shows the object or person as it, he, or she appeared at the time of initial contact. Pictures I and II show objects from a different viewpoint than that of the Subject picture. For example, if the Subject picture presents a front view, I and II may present back views, side views, or a back and a side view. Also, art objects may be displayed differently, may have a different base or frame or method of hanging.

When the subject is a person, I or II will be a picture of a different person or will be a picture of the same person after some change has taken place. The person may have made a deliberate attempt to alter his or her appearance, such as wearing (or taking off a wig, growing (or shaving off) a beard or mustache, or dressing as a member of the opposite sex. The change may also be a natural one, such as changing a hair style, changing from work clothes to play clothes, or from play clothes to work clothes, or growing older, thinner, or fatter. None has had cosmetic surgery.

8 (#1)

7.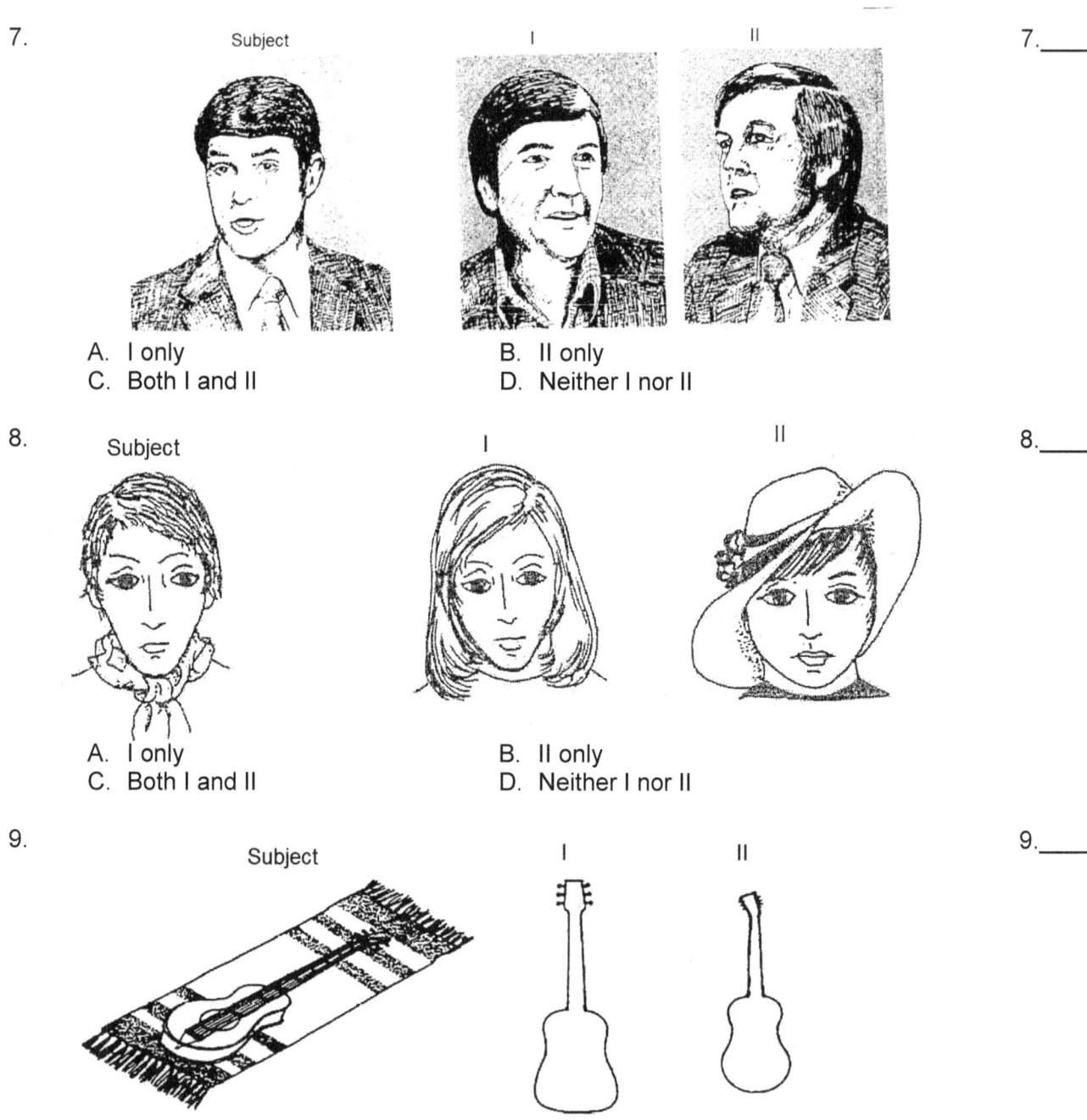

A. I only B. II only
C. Both I and II D. Neither I nor II

7.____

8.
A. I only B. II only
C. Both I and II D. Neither I nor II

8.____

9.
A. I only B. II only
C. Both I and II D. Neither I nor II

9.____

10. Subject   I   II   10.____

  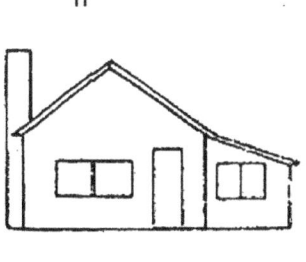

A. I only
B. II only
C. Both I and II
D. Neither I nor II

KEY (CORRECT ANSWERS)

1.	B	6.	B
2.	D	7.	D
3.	A	8.	A
4.	A	9.	D
5.	B	10.	D

PREPARING WRITTEN MATERIAL

PARAGRAPH REARRANGEMENT
COMMENTARY

The sentences that follow are in scrambled order. You are to rearrange them in proper order and indicate the letter choice containing the correct answer at the space at the right.

Each group of sentences in this section is actually a paragraph presented in scrambled order. Each sentence in the group has a place in that paragraph; no sentence is to be left out. You are to read each group of sentences and decide upon the best order in which to put the sentences so as to form a well-organized paragraph.

The questions in this section measure the ability to solve a problem when all the facts relevant to its solution are not given.

More specifically, certain positions of responsibility and authority require the employee to discover connection between events sometimes, apparently, unrelated. In order to do this, the employee will find it necessary to correctly infer that unspecified events have probably occurred or are likely to occur. This ability becomes especially important when action must be taken on incomplete information.

Accordingly, these questions require competitors to choose among several suggested alternatives, each of which presents a different sequential arrangement of the events. Competitors must choose the MOST logical of the suggested sequences.

In order to do so, they may be required to draw on general knowledge to infer missing concepts or events that are essential to sequencing the given events. Competitors should be careful to infer only what is essential to the sequence. The plausibility of the wrong alternatives will always require the inclusion of unlikely events or of additional chains of events which are NOT essential to sequencing the given events.

It's very important to remember that you are looking for the best of the four possible choices, and that the best choice of all may not even be one of the answers you're given to choose from.

There is no one right way to solve these problems. Many people have found it helpful to first write out the order of the sentences, as they would have arranged them, on their scrap paper before looking at the possible answers. If their optimum answer is there, this can save them some time. If it isn't, this method can still give insight into solving the problem. Others find it most helpful to just go through each of the possible choices, contrasting each as they go along. You should use whatever method feels comfortable and works for you.

While most of these types of questions are not that difficult, we've added a higher percentage of the difficult type, just to give you more practice. Usually there are only one or two questions on this section that contain such subtle distinctions that you're unable to answer confidently. And you then may find yourself stuck deciding between two possible choices, neither of which you're sure about.

PREPARING WRITTEN MATERIAL
PARAGRAPH REARRANGEMENT
EXAMINATION SECTION
TEST 1

DIRECTIONS: The sentences that follow are in scrambled order. You are to rearrange them in proper order and indicate the letter choice containing the CORRECT answer. *PRINT THE LETTER OF THE CORRECT ANSWER IN THE SPACE AT THE RIGHT.*

1. Police Officer Jenner responds to the scene of a burglary at 2106 La Vista Boulevard. He is approached by an elderly man named Richard Jenkins, whose account of the incident includes the following five sentences:
    I. I saw that the lock on my apartment door had been smashed and the door was open.
    II. My apartment was a shambles; my belongings were everywhere and my television set was missing.
    III. As I walked down the hallway toward the bedroom, I heard someone opening a window.
    IV. I left work at 5:30 P.M. and took the bus home.
    V. At that time, I called the police.
    The MOST logical order for the above sentence to appear in the report is
    A. I, V, IV, II, III   B. IV, I, II, III, V   C. I, V, II, III, IV   D. IV, III, II, V, I

    1.____

2. Police Officer LaJolla is writing an Incident Report in which back-up assistance was required. The report will contain the following five sentences:
    I. The radio dispatcher asked what my location was and he then dispatched patrol cars for back-up assistance.
    II. At approximately 9:30 P.M., while I was walking my assigned footpost, a gunman fired three shots at me.
    III. I quickly turned around and saw a white male, approximately 5'10", with black hair, wearing blue jeans, a yellow T-shirt, and white sneaker, running across the avenue carrying a handgun.
    IV. When the back-up officers arrived, we searched the area but could not find the suspect.
    V. I advised the radio dispatcher that a gunman had just fired a gun at me, and then I gave the dispatcher a description of the man
    The MOST logical order for the above sentences to appear in the report is:
    A. III, V, II, IV, I   B. II, III, V, I, IV   C. III, II, IV, I, V   D. II, V, I, III, IV

    2.____

3. Police Officer Durant is completing a report of a robbery and assault. The report will contain the following five sentences:
    I. I went to Mount Snow Hospital to interview a man who was attacked and robbed of his wallet earlier that night.
    II. An ambulance arrived at 82nd Street and 3rd Avenue and took an intoxicated, wounded man to Mount Snow Hospital
    III. Two youths attacked the man and stole his wallet.

    3.____

IV. A well-dressed man left Hanratty's Bar very drunk, with his wallet hanging out of his back pocket.
V. A passerby dialed 911 and requested police and ambulance assistance.
The MOST logical order for the above sentences to appear in the report is
   A. I, II, IV, III, V   B. IV, III, V, II, I   C. IV, V, II, III, I   D. V, IV, III, II, I

4. Police Officer Boswell is preparing a report of an armed robbery and assault which will contain the following five sentences:
   I. Both men approached the bartender and one of them drew a gun.
   II. The bartender immediately went to grab the phone at the bar.
   III. One of the men leaped over the counter and smashed a bottle over the bartender's head.
   IV. Two men in a blue Buick drove up to the bar and went inside.
   V. I found the cash register empty and the bartender unconscious on the floor, with the phone still dangling off the hook.
   The MOST logical order for the above sentences to appear in the report is
      A. IV, I, II, III, V   B. V, IV, III, I, II   C. IV, III, II, V, I   D. II, I, III, IV, V

4.____

5. Police Officer Mitzler is preparing a report of a bank robbery, which will contain the following five sentences:
   I. The teller complied with the instructions on the note, but also hit the silent alarm.
   II. The perpetrator then fled south on Broadway.
   III. A suspicious male entered the bank at approximately 10:45 A.M.
   IV. At this time, an undetermined amount of money has been taken.
   V. He approached the teller on the far right side and handed her a note.
   The MOST logical order for the above sentences to appear in the report is:
      A. III, V, I, II, IV   B. I, III, V, II, IV   C. III, V, IV, I, II   D. III, V, II, IV, I

5.____

6. A Police Officer is preparing an Accident Report for an accident which occurred at the intersection of East 119th Street and Lexington Avenue. The report will include the following five sentences:
   I. On September 18, while driving ten children to school, a school bus driver passed out.
   II. Upon arriving at the scene, I notified the dispatcher to send an ambulance.
   III. I notified the parents of each child once I got to the station house.
   IV. He said the school bus, while traveling west on East 119th Street, struck a parked Ford which was on the southwest corner of East 119th Street.
   V. A witness by the name of John Ramos came up to me to describe what happened.
   The MOST logical order for the above sentences to appear in the Accident Report is:
      A. I, II, V, III, IV   B. I, II, V, IV, III   C. II, V, I, III, IV   D. II, V, I, IV, III

6.____

7. A Police Officer is preparing a report concerning a dispute. The report will contain the following five sentences:
   I. The passenger got out of the back of the taxi and leaned through the front window to complain to the driver about the fare.

7.____

II. The driver of the taxi caught up with the passenger and knocked him to the ground; the passenger then kicked the driver and a scuffle ensued.
III. The taxi drew up in front of the high-rise building and stopped.
IV. The driver got out of the taxi and followed the passenger into the lobby of the apartment building.
V. The doorman tried but was unable to break up the fight, at which point he called the precinct.

The MOST logical order for the above sentences to appear in the report is
   A. III, I, IV, II, V   B. III, IV, I, II, V   C. III, IV, II, V, I   D. V, I, III, IV, II

8. Police Officer Morrow is writing an Incident Report. The report will include the following four sentences:
   I. The man reached into his pocket and pulled out a gun.
   II. While on foot patrol, I identified a suspect, who was wanted for six robberies in the area, from a wanted picture I was carrying.
   III. I drew my weapon and fired six rounds at the suspect, killing him instantly.
   IV. I called for back-up assistance and told the man to put his hands up.

   The MOST logical order for the above sentences to appear in the report is
      A. II, III, IV, I   B. IV, I, III, II   C. IV, I, II, III   D. II, IV, I, III

9. Sergeant Allen responds to a call at 16 Grove Street regarding a missing child. At the scene, the Sergeant is met by Police Officer Samuels, who gives a brief account of the incident consisting of the following five sentences:
   I. I transmitted the description and waited for you to arrive before I began searching the area.
   II. Mrs. Banks, the mother, reports that she last saw her daughter Julie about 7:30 A.M. when she took her to school.
   III. About 6 P.M., my partner and I arrived at this location to investigate a report of a missing 8-year-old girl.
   IV. When Mrs. Banks left her, Julie was wearing a red and white striped T-shirt, blue jeans, and white sneakers.
   V. Mrs. Banks dropped her off in front of the playground of P.S. 11.

   The MOST logical order for the above sentences to appear in the report is
      A. III, V, IV, II, I   B. III, II, V, IV, I   C. III, IV, I, II, V   D. III, II, IV, I, V

10. Police Officer Franco is completing a report of an assault. The report will contain the following five sentences:
    I. In the park I observed an elderly man lying on the ground, bleeding from a back wound.
    II. I applied first aid to control the bleeding and radioed for an ambulance to respond.
    III. The elderly man stated that he was sitting on the park bench when he was attacked from behind by two males.
    IV. I received a report of a man's screams coming from inside the park, and I went to investigate.
    V. The old man could not give a description of his attackers.

    The MOST logical order for the above sentences to appear in the report is
       A. IV, I, II, III, V   B. V, III, I, IV, II   C. IV, III, V, II, I   D. II, I, V, IV, III

11. Police Officer Williams is completing a Crime Report. The report contains the following five sentences:
    I. As Police Officer Hanson and I approached the store, we noticed that the front door was broken.
    II. After determining that the burglars had fled, we notified the precinct of the burglary.
    III. I walked through the front door as Police Officer Hanson walked around to the back.
    IV. At approximately midnight, an alarm was heard at the Apex Jewelry Store.
    V. We searched the store and found no one.
    The MOST logical order for the above sentences to appear in the report is
       A. I, IV, II, III, V   B. I, IV, III, V, II   C. IV, I, III, II, V   D. IV, I, III, V, II

12. Police Officer Clay is giving a report to the news media regarding someone who has jumped from the Empire State Building. His report will include the following five sentences:
    I. I responded to the 86th floor, where I found the person at the edge of the roof.
    II. A security guard at the building had reported that a man was on the roof at the 86th floor.
    III. At 5:30 P.M., the person jumped from the building.
    IV. I received a call from the radio dispatcher at 4:50 P.M. to respond to the Empire State Building.
    V. I tried to talk to the person and convince him not to jump.
    The MOST logical order for the above sentences to appear in the report is
       A. I, II, IV, III, V   B. III, IV, I, II, V   C. II, IV, I, III, V   D. IV, II, I, V, III

13. The following five sentences are part of a report of a burglary written by Police Officer Reed:
    I. When I arrived at 2400 1st Avenue, I noticed that the door was slightly open.
    II. I yelled out, *Police, don't move!*
    III. As I entered the apartment, I saw a man with a TV set passing through a window to another man standing on a fire escape.
    IV. While on foot patrol, I was informed by the radio dispatcher that a burglary was in progress at 2400 1st Avenue.
    V. However, the burglars quickly ran down the fire escape.
    The MOST logical order for the above sentences to appear in the report is
       A. I, III, IV, V, II   B. IV, I, III, V, II   C. IV, I, III, II, V   D. I, IV, III, II, V

14. Police Officer Jenkins is preparing a report for Lost or Stolen Property. The report will include the following five sentences:
    I. On the stairs, Mr. Harris slipped on a wet leaf and fell on the landing.
    II. It wasn't until he got to the token booth that Mr. Harris realized his wallet was no longer in his back pants pocket.
    III. A boy wearing a football jersey helped him up and brushed off the back of Mr. Harris' pants.
    IV. Mr. Harris states he was walking up the stairs to the elevated subway at Queensborough Plaza.
    V. Before Mr. Harris could thank him, the boy was running down the stairs to the street.

The MOST logical order for the above sentences to appear in the report is
A. IV, III, V, I, II   B. IV, I, III, V, II   C. I, IV, II, III, V   D. I, II, IV, III, V

15. Police Officer Hubbard is completing a report of a missing person. The report will contain the following five sentences:
I. I visited the store at 7:55 P.M. and asked the employees if they had seen a girl fitting the description I had been given.
II. She gave me a description and said she had gone into the local grocery store at about 6:15 P.M.
III. I asked the woman for a description of her daughter.
IV. The distraught woman called the precinct to report that her daughter, aged 12, had not returned from an errand.
V. The storekeeper said a girl matching the description had been in the store earlier, but he could not give an exact time.
The MOST logical order for the above sentences to appear in the report is
A. I, III, II, V, IV   B. IV, III, II, I, V   C. V, I, II, III, IV   D. III, I, II, IV, V

15.____

16. A police officer is completing an entry in his Daily Activity Log regarding traffic summonses which he issued. The following five sentences will be included in the entry:
I. I was on routine patrol parked 16 yards west of 170th Street and Clay Avenue.
II. The summonses were issued for unlicensed operator and disobeying a steady red light.
III. At 8 A.M. hours, I observed an auto traveling westbound on 170th Street not stop for a steady red light at the intersection of Clay Avenue and 170th Street.
IV. I stopped the driver of the auto and determined that he did not have a valid driver's license.
V. After a brief conversation, I informed the motorist that he was receiving two summonses.
The MOST logical order for the above sentences to appear in the report is
A. I, III, IV, V, II   B. III, IV, II, V, I   C. V, II, I, III, IV   D. IV, V, II, I, III

16.____

17. The following sentences appeared on an Incident Report:
I. Three teenagers who had been ejected from the theater were yelling at patrons who were now entering.
II. Police Officer Dixon told the teenagers to leave the area.
III. The teenager said that they were told by the manager to leave the theater because they were talking during the movie.
IV. The theater manager called the precinct at 10:20 P.M. to report a disturbance outside the theater.
V. A patrol car responded to the theater at 10:42 P.M. and two police officers went over to the teenagers.
The MOST logical order for the above sentences to appear in the Incident Report is
A. I, V, IV, III, II   B. IV, I, V, III, II   C. IV, I, III, V, II   D. IV, III, I, V, II

17.____

18. Activity Log entries are completed by police officers. Police Officer Samuels has written an entry concerning vandalism and part of it contains the following five sentences:
    I. The man, in his early twenties, ran down the block and around the corner.
    II. A man passing the store threw a brick through a window of the store.
    III. I arrived on the scene and began to question the witnesses about the incident.
    IV. Malcolm Holmes, the owner of the Fast Service Shoe Repair Store, was working in the back of the store at approximately 3 P.M.
    V. After the man fled, Mr. Holmes called the police.
    The MOST logical order for the above sentences to appear in the Activity Log is
    A. IV, II, I, V, III   B. II, IV, I, III, V   C. II, I, IV, III, V   D. IV, II, V, III, I

18.____

19. Police Officer Buckley is preparing a report concerning a dispute in a restaurant. The report will contain the following five sentences:
    I. The manager, Charles Chin, and a customer, Edward Green, were standing near the register arguing over the bill.
    II. The manager refused to press any charges providing Green pay the check and leave.
    III. While on foot patrol, I was informed by a passerby of a disturbance in the Dragon Flame Restaurant.
    IV. Green paid the $15.00 check and left the restaurant.
    V. According to witnesses, the customer punched the owner in the face when Chin asked him for the amount due.
    The MOST logical order for the above sentences to appear in the report is
    A. III, I, V, II, IV   B. I, II, III, IV, V   C. V, I, III, II, IV   D. III, V, II, IV, I

19.____

20. Police Officer Wilkins is preparing a report for leaving the scene of an accident. The report will include the following five sentences:
    I. The Dodge struck the right rear fender of Mrs. Smith's 2010 Ford and continued on its way.
    II. Mrs. Smith stated she was making a left turn from 40th Street onto Third Avenue.
    III. As the car passed, Mrs. Smith noticed the dangling rear license plate #412AEJ.
    IV. Mrs. Smith complained to police of back pains and was removed by ambulance to Bellevue Hospital.
    V. An old green Dodge traveling up Third Avenue went through the red light at 40th Street and Third Avenue.
    The MOST logical order for the above sentences to appear in the report is
    A. V, III, I, II, IV   B. I, III, II, V, IV   C. IV, V, I, II, III   D. II, V, I, III, IV

20.____

21. Detective Simon is completing a Crime Report. The report contains the following five sentences:
    I. Police Officer Chin, while on foot patrol, heard the yelling and ran in the direction of the man.
    II. The man, carrying a large hunting knife, left the High Sierra Sporting Goods Store at approximately 10:30 A.M.

21.____

III. When the man heard Police Officer Chin, he stopped, dropped the knife, and began to cry.
IV. As Police Officer Chin approached the man, he drew his gun and yelled, *Police, freeze.*
V. After the man left the store, he began yelling, over and over, *I am going to kill myself!*

The MOST logical order for the above sentences to appear in the report is
   A. V, II, I, IV, III   B. II, V, I, IV, III   C. II, V, IV, I, III   D. II, I, V, IV, III

22. Police Officer Miller is preparing a Complaint Report which will include the following five sentences:
    I. From across the lot, he yelled to the boys to get away from his car.
    II. When he came out of the store, he noticed two teenage boys trying to break into his car.
    III. The boys fled as Mr. Johnson ran to his car.
    IV. Mr. Johnson stated that he parked his car in the municipal lot behind Tams Department Store.
    V. Mr. Johnson saw that the door lock had been broken, but nothing was missing from inside the auto.

    The MOST logical order for the above sentences to appear in the report is
       A. IV, I, II, V, III   B. II, III, I, V, IV   C. IV, II, I, III, V   D. I, II, III, V, IV

22.____

23. Police Officer O'Hara completes a Universal Summons for a motorist who has just passed a red traffic light. The Universal Summons includes the following five sentences:
    I. As the car passed the light, I followed in the patrol car.
    II. After the driver stopped the car, he stated that the light was yellow, not red.
    III. A blue Cadillac sedan passed the red light on the corner of 79th Street and 3rd Avenue at 11:25 P.M.
    IV. As a result, the driver was informed that he did pass a red light and that his brake lights were not working.
    V. The driver in the Cadillac stopped his car as soon as he saw the patrol car, and I noticed that the brake lights were not working.

    The MOST logical order for the above sentences to appear in the Universal Summons is
       A. I, III, V, II, IV   B. III, I, V, II, IV   C. III, I, V, IV, II   D. I, III, IV, II, V

23.____

24. Detective Egan is preparing a follow-up report regarding a homicide on 170th Street and College Avenue. An unknown male was found at the scene. The report will contain the following five sentences:
    I. Police Officer Gregory wrote down the names, addresses, and phone numbers of the witnesses.
    II. A 911 operator received a call of a man shot and dispatched Police Officers Worth and Gregory to the scene.
    III. They discovered an unidentified male dead on the street.
    IV. Police Officer Worth notified the Precinct Detective Unit immediately.
    V. At approximately 9:00 A.M., an unidentified male shot another male in the chest during an argument.

24.____

The MOST logical order for the above sentences to appear in the report is
A. V, II, III, IV, I   B. II, III, V, IV, I   C. IV, I, V, II, III   D. V, III, II, IV, I

25. Police Officer Tracey is preparing a Robbery Report which will include the following five sentences:
    I. I ran around the corner and observe a man pointing a gun at a taxidriver.
    II. I informed the man I was a police officer and that he should not move.
    III. I was on the corner of 125th Street and Park Avenue when I heard a scream coming from around the corner.
    IV. The man turned around and fired one shot at me.
    V. I fired once, shooting him in the arm and causing him to fall to the ground.
    The MOST logical order for the above sentences to appear in the report is
    A. I, III, IV, II, V   B. IV, V, II, I, III   C. III, I, II, IV, V   D. III, I, V, II, IV

KEY (CORRECT ANSWERS)

1.	B		11.	D
2.	B		12.	D
3.	B		13.	C
4.	A		14.	B
5.	A		15.	B
6.	B		16.	A
7.	A		17.	B
8.	D		18.	A
9.	B		19.	A
10.	A		20.	D

21.	B
22.	C
23.	B
24.	A
25.	C

TEST 2

DIRECTIONS: The sentences that follow are in scrambled order. You are to rearrange them in proper order and indicate the letter choice containing the CORRECT answer. *PRINT THE LETTER OF THE CORRECT ANSWER IN THE SPACE AT THE RIGHT*

1. Police Officer Weiker is completing a Complaint Report which will contain the following five sentences:
   I. Mr. Texlor was informed that the owner of the van would receive a parking ticket and that the van would be towed away.
   II. The police tow truck arrived approximately one half hour after Mr. Texlor complained.
   III. While on foot patrol on West End Avenue, I saw the owner of Rand's Restaurant arrive to open his business.
   IV. Mr. Texlor, the owner, called to me and complained that he could not receive deliveries because a van was blocking his driveway.
   V. The van's owner later reported to the precinct that his van had been stolen, and he was then informed that it had been towed.
   The MOST logical order for the above sentences to appear in the report is
     A. III, V, I, II, IV   B. III, IV, I, II, V   C. IV, III, I, II, V   D. IV, III, II, I, V

   1._____

2. Police Officer Ames is completing an entry in his Activity Log. The entry contains the following five sentences:
   I. Mr. Sands gave me a complete description of the robber.
   II. Alvin Sands, owner of the Star Delicatessen, called the precinct to report he had just been robbed.
   III. I then notified all police patrol vehicles to look for a white male in his early twenties wearing brown pants and shirt, a black leather jacket, and black and white sneakers.
   IV. I arrived on the scene after being notified by the precinct that a robbery had just occurred at the Star Delicatessen.
   V. Twenty minutes later, a man fitting the description was arrested by a police officer on patrol six blocks from the delicatessen.
   The MOST logical order for the above sentences to appear in the Activity Log is
     A. II, I, IV, III, V   B. II IV, III, I, V   C. II, IV, I, III, V   D. II, IV, I, V, III

   2._____

3. Police Officer Benson is completing a Complaint Report concerning a stolen taxicab, which will include the following five sentences:
   I. Police Officer Benson noticed that a cab was parked next to a fire hydrant.
   II. Dawson *borrowed* the cab for transportation purposes since he was in a hurry.
   III. Ed Dawson got into his car and tried to start it, but the battery was dead.
   IV. When he reached his destination, he parked the cab by a fire hydrant and placed the keys under the seat.
   V. He looked around and saw an empty cab with the engine running.
   The MOST logical order for the above sentences to appear in the report is
     A. I, III, II, IV, V   B. III, I, II, V, IV   C. III, V, II, IV, I   D. V, II, IV, III, I

   3._____

4. Police Officer Hatfield is reviewing his Activity Log entry prior to completing a report. The entry contains the following five sentences:
   I. When I arrived at Zand's Jewelry Store, I noticed that the door was slightly open.
   II. I told the burglar I was a police officer and that he should stand still or he would be shot.
   III. As I entered the store, I saw a man wearing a ski mask attempting to open the safe in the back of the store.
   IV. On December 16, 2020, at 1:38 A.M., I was informed that a burglary was in progress at Zand's Jewelry Store on East 59th Street.
   V. The burglar quickly pulled a knife from his pocket when he saw me.
   The MOST logical order for the above sentences to appear in the report is
   A. IV, I, III, V, II   B. I, IV, III, V, II   C. IV, III, II, V, I   D. I, III, IV, V, II

5. Police Officer Lorenz is completing a report of a murder. The report will contain the following five statements made by a witness:
   I. I was awakened by the sound of a gunshot coming from the apartment next door and I decided to check.
   II. I entered the apartment and looked into the kitchen and the bathroom.
   III. I found Mr. Hubbard's body slumped in the bathtub.
   IV. The door to the apartment was open, but I didn't see anyone.
   V. He had been shot in the head.
   The MOST logical order for the above sentences to appear in the report is
   A. I, III, II, IV, V   B. I, IV, II, III, V   C. IV, II, I, III, V   D. III, I, II, IV, V

6. Police Officer Baldwin is preparing an accident report which will include the following five sentences:
   I. The old man lay on the ground for a few minutes, but was not physically hurt.
   II. Charlie Watson, a construction worker, was repairing some brick work at the top of a building at 54th Street and Madison Avenue.
   III. Steven Green, his partner, warned him that this could be dangerous, but Watson ignored him.
   IV. A few minutes later, one of the bricks thrown by Watson smashed to the ground in front of an old man, who fainted out of fright.
   V. Mr. Watson began throwing some of the bricks over the side of the building.
   The MOST logical order for the above sentences to appear in the report is
   A. II, V, III, IV, I   B. I, IV, II, V, III   C. III, II, IV, V, I   D. II, III, I, IV, V

7. Police Officer Porter is completing an Incident Report concerning her rescue of a woman being held hostage by a former boyfriend. Her report will contain the following five sentences:
   I. I saw a man holding .25 caliber gun to a woman's head, but he did not see me.
   II. I then broke a window and gained access to the house.
   III. As I approached the house on foot, a gunshot rang out and I heard a woman scream.
   IV. A decoy van brought me as close as possible to the house where the woman was being held hostage.

V. I ordered the man to drop his gun, and he released the woman and was taken into custody.

The MOST logical order for the above sentences to appear in the report is
   A. I, III, II, IV, V   B. IV, III, II, I, V   C. III, II, I, IV, V   D. V, I, II, III, IV

8. Police Officer Byrnes is preparing a crime report concerning a robbery. The report will consist of the following five sentences:
    I. Mr. White, following the man's instructions, opened the car's hood, at which time the man got out of the auto, drew a revolver, and ordered White to give him all the money in his pockets.
    II. Investigation has determined there were no witnesses to this incident.
    III. The man asked White to check the oil and fill the tank.
    IV. Mr. White, a gas attendant, states that he was working alone at the gas station when a black male pulled up to the gas pump in a white Mercury.
    V. White was then bound and gagged by the male and locked in the gas station's rest room.

    The MOST logical order for the above sentences to appear in the report is
       A. IV, I, III, II, V   B. III, I, II, V, IV   C. IV, III, I, V, II   D. I, III, IV, II, V

9. Police Officer Gale is preparing a report of a crime committed against Mr. Weston. The report will consist of the following five sentences:
    I. The man, who had a gun, told Mr. Weston not to scream for help and ordered him back into the apartment.
    II. With Mr. Weston disposed of in this fashion, the man proceeded to ransack the apartment.
    III. Opening the door to see who was there, Mr. Weston was confronted by a tall white male wearing a dark blue jacket and white pants.
    IV. Mr. Weston was at home alone in his living room when the doorbell rang.
    V. Once inside, the man bound and gagged Mr. Weston and locked him in the bathroom.

    The MOST logical order for the above sentences to appear in the report is
       A. III, V, II, I, IV   B. IV, III, I, V, II   C. III, V, IV, II, I   D. IV, III, V, I, II

10. A police officer is completing a report of a robbery, which will contain the following five sentences:
    I. Two police officers were about to enter the Red Rose Coffee Shop on 47th Street and 8th Avenue.
    II. They then noticed a male running up the street carrying a brown paper bag.
    III. They heard a woman standing outside the Broadway Boutique yelling that her store had just been robbed by a young man, and she was pointing up the street.
    IV. They caught up with him and made an arrest.
    V. The police officers pursued the male, who ran past them on 8th Avenue.

    The MOST logical order for the above sentences to appear in the report is
       A. I, III, II, V, IV   B. III, I, II, V, IV   C. IV, V, I, II, III   D. I, V, IV, III, II

11. Police Officer Capalbo is preparing a report of a bank robbery. The report will contain the following five statements made by a witness:
    I. Initialing, all I could see were two men, dressed in maintenance uniforms, sitting in the area reserved for bank officers.
    II. I was passing the bank at 8 P.M. and noticed that all the lights were out, except in the rear section.
    III. Then I noticed two other men in the bank, coming from the direction of the vault, carrying a large metal box.
    IV. At this point, I decided to call the police.
    V. I knocked on the window to get the attention of the men in the maintenance uniforms, and they chased the two men carrying the box down a flight of steps.
    The MOST logical order for the above sentences to appear in the report is
        A. IV, I, II, V, III   B. I, III, II, V, IV   C. II, I, III, V, IV   D. II, III, I, V, IV

12. Police Officer Roberts is preparing a crime report concerning an assault and a stolen car. The report will contain the following five sentences:
    I. Upon leaving the store to return to his car, Winters noticed that a male unknown to him was sitting in his car.
    II. The man then re-entered Winters' car and drove away, fleeing north on 2nd Avenue.
    III. Mr. Winters stated that he parked his car in front of 235 East 25th Street and left the engine running while he went into the butcher shop at that location.
    IV. Mr. Robert Gering, a witness, stated that the male is known in the neighborhood as Bobby Rae and is believed to reside at 323 East 114th Street.
    V. When Winters approached the car and ordered the man to get out, the man got out of the auto and struck Winters with his fists, knocking him to the ground.
    The MOST logical order for the above sentences to appear in the report is
        A. III, II, V, I, IV   B. III, I, V, II, IV   C. I, IV, V, II, III   D. III, II, I, V, IV

13. Police Officer Robinson is preparing a crime report concerning the robbery of Mr. Edwards' store. The report will consist of the following five sentences:
    I. When the last customer left the store, the two men drew revolvers and ordered Mr. Edwards to give them all the money in the cash register.
    II. The men proceeded to the back of the store as if they were going to do some shopping.
    III. Janet Morley, a neighborhood resident, later reported that she saw the men enter a green Ford station wagon and flee northbound on Albany Avenue.
    IV. Edwards complied after which the gunmen ran from the store.
    V. Mr. Edwards states that he was stocking merchandise behind the store counter when two white males entered the store.
    The MOST logical order for the above sentences to appear in the report is
        A. V, II, III, I, IV   B. V, II, I, IV, III   C. II, I, V, IV, III   D. III, V, II, I, IV

14. Police Officer Wendell is preparing an accident report for a 6-car accident that occurred at the intersection of Bath Avenue and Bay Parkway. The report will consist of the following five sentences:
    I. A 2016 Volkswagen Beetle, traveling east on Bath Avenue, swerved to the left to avoid the Impala, and struck a 2014 Ford station wagon which was traveling west on Bath Avenue.
    II. The Seville then mounted the curb on the northeast corner of Bath Avenue and Bay Parkway and struck a light pole.
    III. A 2013 Buick Lesabre, traveling northbound on Bay Parkway directly behind the Impala, struck the Impala, pushing it into the intersection of Bath Avenue and Bay Parkway.
    IV. A 2015 Chevy Impala, traveling northbound on Bay Parkway, had stopped for a red light at Bath Avenue.
    V. A 2017 Toyota, traveling westbound on Bath Avenue, swerved to the right to avoid hitting the Ford station wagon, and struck a 2017 Cadillac Seville double-parked near the corner.
    The MOST logical order for the above sentences to appear in the report is
    A. IV, III, V, II, I   B. III, IV, V, II, I   C. IV, III, I, V, II   D. III, IV, V, I, II

15. The following five sentences are part of an Activity Log entry Police Officer Rogers made regarding an explosion:
    I. I quickly treated the pedestrian for the injury.
    II. The explosion caused a glass window in an office building to shatter.
    III. After the pedestrian was treated, a call was placed to the precinct requesting additional police officers to evacuate the area.
    IV. After all the glass settled to the ground, I saw a pedestrian who was bleeding from the arm.
    V. While on foot patrol near 5th Avenue and 53rd Street, I heard a loud explosion.
    The MOST logical order for the above sentences to appear in the report is
    A. II, V, IV, I, III   B. V, II, IV, III, I   C. V, II, I, IV, III   D. V, II, IV, I, III

16. Police Officer David is completing a report regarding illegal activity near the entrance to Madison Square Garden during a recent rock concert. The report will obtain the following five sentences:
    I. As I came closer to the man, he placed what appeared to be tickets in his pocket and began to walk away.
    II. After the man stopped, I questioned him about *scalping* tickets.
    III. While on assignment near the Madison Square Garden entrance, I observed a man apparently selling tickets.
    IV. I stopped the man by stating that I was a police officer.
    V. The man was then given a summons, and he left the area.
    The MOST logical order for the above sentences to appear in the report is
    A. I, III, IV, II, V   B. III, I, IV, V, II   C. III, IV, I, II, V   D. III, I, IV, II, V

17. Police Officer Sampson is preparing a report containing a dispute in a bar. The report will contain the following five sentences:
    I. John Evans, the bartender, ordered the two men out of the bar.
    II. Two men dressed in dungarees entered the C and D Bar at 5:30 P.M.
    III. The two men refused to leave and began to beat up Evans.
    IV. A customer in the bar saw me on patrol and yelled to me to come separate the three men.
    V. The two men became very drunk and loud within a short time.
    The MOST logical order for the above sentences to appear in the report is
    A. II, I, V, III, IV   B. II, III, IV, V, I   C. III, I, II, V, IV   D. II, V, I, III, IV

18. A police officer is completing a report concerning the response to a crime in progress. The report will include the following five sentences:
    I. The officers saw two armed men run out of the liquor store and into a waiting car.
    II. Police Officers Lunty and Duren received the call and responded to the liquor store.
    III. The robbers gave up without a struggle.
    IV. Lunty and Duren blocked the getaway car with their patrol car.
    V. A call came into the precinct concerning a robbery in progress at Jane's Liquor Store.
    The MOST logical order for the above sentence to appear in the report is
    A. V, II, I, IV, III   B. II, V, I, III, IV   C. V, I, IV, II, III   D. I, V, II, III, IV

19. Police Officers Jenkins is preparing a Crime Report which will consist of the following five sentences:
    I. After making inquirie in the vicinity, Smith found out that his next door neighbor, Viola Jones, had seen two local teenagers, Michael Heinz and Vincent Gaynor, smash his car's windshields with a crowbar.
    II. Jones told Smith that the teenagers live at 8700 19th Avenue.
    III. Mr. Smith heard a loud crash at approximately 11:00 P.M., looked out of his apartment window, and saw two white males running away from his car.
    IV. Smith then reported the incident to the precinct, and Heinz and Gaynor were arrested at the address given.
    V. Leaving his apartment to investigate further, Smith discovered that his car's front and rear windshields had been smashed.
    The MOST logical order for the above sentences to appear in the report is
    A. III, IV, V, I, II   B. III, V, I, II, IV   C. III, I, V, II, IV   D. V, III, I, II, IV

20. Sergeant Nancy Winston is reviewing a Gun Control Report which will contain the following five sentences:
    I. The man fell to the floor when hit in the chest with three bullets from 22 caliber gun.
    II. Merriam's 22 caliber gun was seized, and he was given a summons for not having a pistol permit.
    III. Christopher Merriam, the owner of A-Z Grocery, shot a man who attempted to rob him.
    IV. Police Officer Franks responded and asked Merriam for his pistol permit, which he could not produce.

V. Merriam phoned the police to report he had just shot a man who had attempted to rob him.

The MOST logical order for the above sentences to appear in the report is
   A. III, I, V, IV, II   B. I, III, V, IV, II   C. III, I, V, II, IV   D. I, III, II, V, IV

21. Detective John Manville is completing a report for his superior regarding the murder of an unknown male who was shot in Central Park. The report will contain the following five sentences:
   I. Police Officers Langston and Cavers responded to the scene.
   II. I received the assignment to investigate the murder in Central Park from Detective Sergeant Rogers.
   III. Langston notified the Detective Bureau after questioning Jason.
   IV. An unknown male, apparently murdered, was discovered in Central Park by Howard Jason, a park employee, who immediately called the police.
   V. Langston and Cavers questioned Jason.

The MOST logical order for the above sentences to appear in the report is
   A. I, IV, V, III, II   B. IV, I, V, II, III   C. IV, I, V, III, II   D. IV, V, I, III, II

22. A police officer is completing a report concerning the arrest of a juvenile. The report will contain the following five sentences:
   I. Sanders then telephoned Jay's parents from the precinct to inform them of their son's arrest.
   II. The store owner resisted, and Jay then shot him and ran from the store.
   III. Jay was transported directly to the precinct by Officer Sanders.
   IV. James Jay, a juvenile, walked into a candy store and announced a hold-up.
   V. Police Officer Sanders, while on patrol, arrested Jay a block from the candy store.

The MOST logical order for the above sentences to appear in the report is
   A. IV, V, II, I, III   B. IV, II, V, III, I   C. II, IV, V, III, I   D. V, IV, II, I, III

23. Police Officer Olsen prepared a crime report for a robbery which contained the following five sentences:
   I. Mr. Gordon was approached by this individual who then produced a gun and demanded the money from the cash register.
   II. The man then fled from the scene on foot, southbound on 5th Avenue.
   III. Mr. Gordon was working at the deli counter when a white male, 5'6", 150-160 lbs., wearing a green jacket and blue pants, entered the store.
   IV. Mr. Gordon complied with the man's demands and handed him the daily receipts.
   V. Further investigation has determined there are no other witnesses to this robbery.

The MOST logical order for the above sentences to appear in the report is
   A. I, III, IV, V, II   B. I, IV, II, III, V   C. III, IV, I, V, II   D. III, I, IV, II, V

24. Police Officer Bryant responded to 285 E. 31st Street to take a crime report of a burglary of Mr. Bond's home. The report will contain a brief description of the incident, consisting of the following five sentences:
   I. When Mr. Bond attempted to stop the burglar by grabbing him, he was pushed to the floor.
   II. The burglar had apparently gained access to the home by forcing open the 2nd floor bedroom window facing the fire escape.
   III. Mr. Bond sustained a head injury in the scuffle, and the burglar exited the home through the front door.
   IV. Finding nothing in the dresser, the burglar proceeded downstairs to the first floor, where he was confronted by Mr. Bond who was reading in the dining room.
   V. Once inside, he searched the drawers of the bedroom dresser.
   The MOST logical order for the above sentences to appear in the report is
      A. V, IV, I, II, III   B. II, V, IV, I, III   C. II, IV, V, III, I   D. III, II, I, V, IV

25. Police Officer Derringer responded to a call of a rape-homicide case in his patrol area and was ordered to prepare an incident report, which will contain the following five sentences:
   I. He pushed Miss Scott to the ground and forcibly raped her.
   II. Mary Scott was approached from behind by a white male, 5'7", 150-160 lbs. wearing dark pants and a white jacket.
   III. As Robinson approached the male, he ordered him to stop.
   IV. Screaming for help, Miss Scott alerted one John Robinson, a local grocer, who chased her assailant as he fled the scene.
   V. The male turned and fired two shots at Robinson, who fell to the ground mortally wounded.
   The MOST logical order for the above sentences to appear in the report is
      A. IV, III, I, II, V   B. II, IV, III, V, I   C. II, IV, I, V, III   D. II, I, IV, III, V

KEY (CORRECT ANSWERS)

1. B
2. C
3. C
4. A
5. B

6. A
7. B
8. C
9. B
10. A

11. C
12. B
13. B
14. C
15. D

16. D
17. D
18. A
19. B
20. A

21. C
22. B
23. D
24. B
25. D

NAME AND NUMBER COMPARISONS

COMMENTARY

This test seeks to measure your ability and disposition to do a job carefully and accurately, your attention to exactness and preciseness of detail, your alertness and versatility in discerning similarities and differences between things, and your power in systematically handling written language symbols.

It is actually a test of your ability to do academic and/or clerical work, using the basic elements of verbal (qualitative) and mathematical (quantitative) learning—words and numbers.

EXAMINATION SECTION

TEST 1

DIRECTIONS: In each line across the page there are three names or numbers that are much alike. Compare the three names or numbers and decide which ones are exactly alike. *PRINT IN THE SPACE AT THE RIGHT THE LETTER:*
  A. if all THREE names or numbers are exactly alike
  B. if only the FIRST and SECOND names or numbers are ALIKE
  C. if only the FIRST and THIRD names or numbers are alike
  D. if only the SECOND or THIRD names or numbers are alike
  E. if ALL THREE names or numbers are DIFFERENT

1.	Davis Hazen	David Hozen	David Hazen	1.____
2.	Lois Appel	Lois Appel	Lois Apfel	2.____
3.	June Allan	Jane Allan	Jane Allan	3.____
4.	10235	10235	10235	4.____
5.	32614	32164	32614	5.____

TEST 2

1.	2395890	2395890	2395890	1.____
2.	1926341	1926347	1926314	2.____
3.	E. Owens McVey	E. Owen McVey	E. Owen McVay	3.____
4.	Emily Neal Rouse	Emily Neal Rowse	Emily Neal Rowse	4.____
5.	H. Merritt Audubon	H. Merriott Audubon	H. Merritt Audubon	5.____

TEST 3

1.	6219354	6219354	6219354	1.____
2.	231793	2312793	2312793	2.____
3.	1065407	1065407	1065047	3.____
4.	Francis Ransdell	Frances Ramsdell	Francis Ramsdell	4.____
5.	Cornelius Detwiler	Cornelius Detwiler	Cornelius Detwiler	5.____

TEST 4

1.	6452054	6452564	6542054	1.____
2.	8501268	8501268	8501286	2.____
3.	Ella Burk Newham	Ella Burk Newnham	Elena Burk Newnham	3.____
4.	Jno. K. Ravencroft	Jno. H. Ravencroft	Jno. H. Ravencoft	4.____
5.	Martin Wills Pullen	Martin Wills Pulen	Martin Wills Pullen	5.____

TEST 5

1.	3457988	3457986	3457986	1.____
2.	4695682	4695862	4695682	2.____
3.	Stricklund Kaneydy	Sticklund Kanedy	Stricklund Kanedy	3.____
4.	Joy Harlor Witner	Joy Harloe Witner	Joy Harloe Witner	4.____
5.	R.M.O. Uberroth	R.M.O. Uberroth	R.N.O. Uberroth	5.____

TEST 6

1. 1592514 — 1592574 — 1592574 — 1.____
2. 2010202 — 2010202 — 2010220 — 2.____
3. 6177396 — 6177936 — 6177396 — 3.____
4. Drusilla S. Ridgeley — Drusilla S. Ridgeley — Drusilla S. Ridgeley — 4.____
5. Andrei I. Tooumantzev — Andrei I. Tourmantzev — Andrei I. Toumantzov — 5.____

TEST 7

1. 5261383 — 5261383 — 5261338 — 1.____
2. 8125690 — 8126690 — 8125609 — 2.____
3. W.E. Johnston — W.E. Johnson — W.E. Johnson — 3.____
4. Vergil L. Muller — Vergil L. Muller — Vergil L. Muller — 4.____
5. Atherton R. Warde — Asheton R. Warde — Atherton P. Warde — 5.____

TEST 8

1. 013469.5 — 023469.5 — 02346.95 — 1.____
2. 33376 — 333766 — 333766 — 2.____
3. Ling-Temco-Vought — Ling-Tenco-Vought — Ling-Temco Vought — 3.____
4. Lorilard Corp. — Lorillard Corp. — Lorrilard Corp. — 4.____
5. American Agronomics Corporation — American Agronomics Corporation — American Agronomic Corporation — 5.____

TEST 9

1.	436592864	436592864	436592864	1.____
2.	197765123	197755123	197755123	2.____
3.	Dewaay Cortvriendt International S.A.	Deway Cortvriendt International S.A.	Deway Corturiendt International S.A.	3.____
4.	Crédit Lyonnais	Crèdit Lyonnais	Crèdit Lyonais	4.____
5.	Algemene Bank Nederland N.V.	Algamene Bank Nederland N.V.	Algemene Bank Naderland N.V.	5.____

TEST 10

1.	00032572	0.0032572	00032522	1.____
2.	399745	399745	398745	2.____
3.	Banca Privata Finanziaria S.p.A.	Banca Privata Finanzaria S.P.A.	Banca Privata Finanziaria S.P.A.	3.____
4.	Eastman Dillon, Union Securities & Co.	Eastman Dillon, Union Securities Co.	Eastman Dillon, Union Securities & Co.	4.____
5.	Arnhold and S. Bleichroeder, Inc.	Arnhold & S. Bleichroeder, Inc.	Arnold and S. Bleichroeder, Inc.	5.____

TEST 11

DIRECTIONS: Answer the questions below on the basis of the following instructions: For each such numbered set of names, addresses, and numbers listed in Columns I and II, select your answer from the following options:
A. The names in Columns I and II are different
B. The addresses in Columns I and II are different
C. The numbers in Columns I and II are different
D. The names, addresses and numbers are identical

1. Francis Jones
    62 Stately Avenue
    96-12446

    Francis Jones
    62 Stately Avenue
    96-21446

    1.____

2. Julio Montez
    19 Ponderosa Road
    56-73161

    Julio Montez
    19 Ponderosa Road
    56-71361

    2.____

3. Mary Mitchell
    2314 Melbourne Drive
    68-92172

    Mary Mitchell
    2314 Melbourne Drive
    68-92172

    3.____

4. Harry Patterson
    25 Dunne Street
    14-33430

    Harry Patterson
    25 Dunne Street
    14-34330

    4.____

5. Patrick Murphy
    171 West Hosmer Street
    93-81214

    Patrick Murphy
    171 West Hosmer Street
    93-18214

    5.____

TEST 12

1. August Schultz
   816 St. Clair Avenue
   53-40149

   August Schultz
   816 St. Claire Avenue
   53-40149

   1.____

2. George Taft
   72 Runnymede Street
   47-04033

   George Taft
   72 Runnymede Street
   47-04023

   2.____

3. Angus Henderson
   1418 Madison Street
   81-76375

   Angus Henderson
   1418 Madison Street
   81-76375

   3.____

4. Carolyn Mazur
   12 Rivenlew Road
   38-99615

   Carolyn Mazur
   12 Rivervane Road
   38-99615

   4.____

5. Adele Russell
   1725 Lansing Lane
   72-91962

   Adela Russell
   1725 Lansing Lane
   72-91962

   5.____

TEST 13

DIRECTIONS: The following questions are based on the instructions given below. In each of the following questions, the 3-line name and address in Column I is the masterlist entry, and the 3-line entry in Column II is the information to be checked against the master list.
If there is one line that is NOT exactly alike, mark your answer A.
If there are two lines NOT exactly alike, mark your answer B.
If there are three lines NOT exactly alike, mark your answer C.
If the lines ALL are exactly alike, mark your answer D.

1. Jerome A. Jackson
   1243 14th Avenue
   New York, N.Y. 10023

   Jerome A. Johnson
   1234 14th Avenue
   New York, N.Y. 10023

   1.____

2. Sophie Strachtheim
   33-28 Connecticut Ave.
   Far Rockaway, N.Y. 11697

   Sophie Strachtheim
   33-28 Connecticut Ave.
   Far Rockaway, N.Y. 11697

   2.____

3. Elisabeth NT. Gorrell
   256 Exchange St
   New York, N.Y. 10013

   Elizabeth NT. Correll
   256 Exchange St.
   New York, N.Y. 10013

   3.____

4. Maria J. Gonzalez
   7516 E. Sheepshead Rd.
   Brooklyn, N.Y. 11240

   Maria J. Gonzalez
   7516 N. Shepshead Rd.
   Brooklyn, N.Y. 11240

   4.____

5. Leslie B. Brautenweiler
   21-57A Seller Terr.
   Flushing, N.Y. 11367

   Leslie B. Brautenwieler
   21-75ASeiler Terr.
   Flushing, N.J. 11367

   5.____

KEY (CORRECT ANSWERS)

TEST 1	TEST 2	TEST 3	TEST 4	TEST 5	TEST 6	TEST 7
1. E	1. A	1. A	1. E	1. D	1. D	1. B
2. B	2. E	2. A	2. B	2. C	2. B	2. E
3. D	3. E	3. B	3. E	3. E	3. C	3. D
4. A	4. D	4. E	4. E	4. D	4. A	4. A
5. C	5. C	5. A	5. C	5. B	5. E	5. E

TEST 8	TEST 9	TEST 10	TEST 11	TEST 12	TEST 13
1. E	1. A	1. E	1. C	1. B	1. B
2. D	2. D	2. B	2. C	2. C	2. D
3. E	3. E	3. E	3. D	3. D	3. A
4. E	4. E	4. C	4. C	4. B	4. A
5. B	5. E	5. E	5. C	5. A	5. C

NAME AND NUMBER CHECKING
EXAMINATION SECTION
TEST 1

DIRECTIONS: This test is designed to measure your speed/and accuracy. You are urged to work both quickly and accurately and to do correctly as many lists as you can in the time allowed. The test consists of lists or pairs of names and numbers. Count the number of IDENTICAL pairs in each list. Then, select the correct number, 1, 2, 3, 4, 5, and indicate your choice in the space at the right. Two sample questions are presented for your guidance, together with the correct solutions.

SAMPLE LIST A
Adelphi College – Adelphia College
Braxton Corp – Braxeton Corp.
Wassaic State School – Wassaic State School
Central Islip State Hospital – Central Isllip State Hospital
Greenwich House – Greenwich House

NOTE: There are only two correct pairs—Wassaic State School and Greenwich House. Therefore, the CORRECT answer is 2.

SAMPLE LIST B
78453694 – 78453684
784530 – 784530
533 – 534
67845 – 67845
2368745 – 2368755

NOTE: There are only two correct pairs—784530 and 67845. Therefore, the CORRECT answer is 2.

LIST 1   1.____
    Diagnostic Clinic   – Diagnostic Clinic
    Yorkville Health   – Yorkville Health
    Meinhard Clinic   – Meinhart Clinic
    Corlears Clinic   – Carlears Clinic
    Tremont Diagnostic   – Tremont Diagnostic

LIST 2   2.____
    73526   – 73526
    7283627198   – 7283627198
    627   – 637
    728352617283   – 7283526178282
    6281   – 6281

2 (#1)

LIST 3   3.____
- Jefferson Clinic — Jeffersen Clinic
- Mott Haven Center — Mott Havan Center
- Bronx Hospital — Bronx Hospital
- Montefiore Hospital — Montifeore Hospital
- Beth Isreal Hospital — Beth Israel Hospital

LIST 4   4.____
- 936271826 — 936371826
- 5271 — 5291
- 82637192037 — 82637192037
- 527182 — 5271882
- 726354256 — 72635456

LIST 5   5.____
- Trinity Hospital — Trinity Hospital
- Central Harlem — Centrel Harlem
- St. Luke's Hospital — St. Lukes' Hospital
- Mt. Sinai Hospital — Mt. Sinia Hospital
- N.Y. Dispensery — N.Y. Dispensary

LIST 6   6.____
- 725361552637 — 725361555637
- 7526378 — 7526377
- 6975 — 6975
- 82637481028 — 82637481028
- 3427 — 3429

LIST 7   7.____
- Misericordia Hospital — Miseracordia Hospital
- Lebonan Hospital — Lebanon Hospital
- Gouverneur Hospital — Gouverner Hospital
- German Polyclinic — German Policlinic
- French Hospital — French Hospital

LIST 8   8.____
- 8277364933251 — 827364933351
- 63728 — 63728
- 367281 — 367281
- 62733846273 — 6273846293
- 62836 — 6283

LIST 9   9.____
- King's County Hospital — Kings County Hospital
- St. Johns Long Island — St. John's Long Island
- Bellevue Hospital — Bellvue Hospital
- Beth David Hospital — Beth David Hospital
- Samaritan Hospital — Samariton Hospital

LIST 10
62836454   – 62836455
42738267   – 42738369
573829   – 573829
738291627874   – 738291627874
725   - 735

10.____

LIST 11
Bloomingdal Clinic   – Bloomingdale Clinic
Communitty Hospital   – Community Hospital
Metroplitan Hospital   – Metropoliton Hospital
Lenox Hill Hospital   – Lonex Hill Hospital
Lincoln Hospital   – Lincoln Hospital

11.____

LIST 12
6283364728   – 6283648
627385   – 627383
54283902   – 54283602
63354   – 63354
7283562781   - 7283562781

12.____

LIST 13
Sydenham Hospital   – Sydanham Hospital
Roosevalt Hospital   – Roosevelt Hospital
Vanderbilt Clinic   – Vanderbild Clinic
Women's Hospital   – Woman's Hospital
Flushing Hospital   – Flushing Hospital

13.____

LIST 14
62738   – 62738
727355542321   – 72735542321
263849332   – 263849332
262837   – 263837
47382912   - 47382922

14.____

LIST 15
Episcopal Hospital   – Episcapal Hospital
Flower Hospital   – Flouer Hospital
Stuyvesent Clinic   – Stuyvesant Clinic
Jamaica Clinic   – Jamaica Clinic
Ridgwood Clinic   – Ridgewood Clinic

15.____

LIST 16
628367299   – 628367399
111   – 111
118293304829   – 1182839489
4448   – 4448
333693678   - 333693678

16.____

4 (#1)

LIST 17   17._____
    Arietta Crane Farm   – Areitta Crane Farm
    Bikur Chilim Home   – Bikur Chilom Home
    Burke Foundation   – Burke Foundation
    Blythedale Home   – Blythdale Home
    Campbell Cottages   – Cambell Cottages

LIST 18   18._____
    32123   – 32132
    273893326783   – 27389326783
    473829   – 473829
    7382937   – 7383937
    3628890122332   - 36289012332

LIST 19   19._____
    Caraline Rest   – Caroline Rest
    Loreto Rest   – Loretto Rest
    Edgewater Creche   – Edgwater Creche
    Holiday Farm   – Holiday Farm
    House of St. Giles   – House of st. Giles

LIST 20   20._____
    557286777   – 55728677
    3678902   – 3678892
    1567839   – 1567839
    7865434712   – 7865344712
    9927382   - 9927382

LIST 21   21._____
    Isabella Home   – Isabela Home
    James A. Moore Home   – James A. More Home
    The Robin's Nest   – The Roben's Nest
    Pelham Home   – Pelam Home
    St. Eleanora's Home   – St. Eleanora's Home

LIST 22   22._____
    273648293048   – 273648293048
    334   – 334
    7362536478   – 7362536478
    7362819273   – 7362819273
    7362   - 7363

LIST 23   23._____
    St. Pheobe's Mission   – St. Phebe's Mission
    Seaside Home   – Seaside Home
    Speedwell Society   – Speedwell Society
    Valeria Home   – Valera Home
    Wiltwyck   - Wildwyck

LIST 24
 63728   – 63738
 63728192736   – 63728192738
 428   – 458
 62738291527   – 62738291529
 63728192   - 63728192

24.____

LIST 25
 McGaffin   – McGafin
 David Ardslee   – David Ardslee
 Axton Supply   – Axeton Supply Co
 Alice Russell   – Alice Russell
 Dobson Mfg. Co.   – Dobsen Mfg. Co.

25.____

KEY (CORRECT ANSWERS)

1.	3		11.	1
2.	3		12.	2
3.	1		13.	1
4.	1		14.	2
5.	1		15.	1
6.	2		16.	3
7.	1		17.	1
8.	2		18.	1
9.	1		19.	1
10.	2		20.	2

21.	1
22.	4
23.	2
24.	1
25.	2

TEST 2

DIRECTIONS: This test is designed to measure your speed/and accuracy. You are urged to work both quickly and accurately and to do correctly as many lists as you can in the time allowed. The test consists of lists or pairs of names and numbers. Count the number of IDENTICAL pairs in each list. Then, select the correct number, 1, 2, 3, 4, 5, and indicate your choice in the space at the right.

LIST 1   1._____
    82637381028   – 82637281028
    928   – 928
    72937281028   – 72937281028
    7362   – 7362
    927382615   – 927382615

LIST 2   2._____
    Albee Theatre   – Albee Theatre
    Lapland Lumber Co.   – Laplund Lumber Co.
    Adelphi College   – Adelphi College
    Jones & Son Inc.   – Jones & Sons Inc.
    S.W. Ponds Co.   – S.W. Ponds Co.

LIST 3   3._____
    85345   – 85345
    895643278   – 895643277
    726352   – 726353
    632685   – 632685
    7263524   – 7236524

LIST 4   4._____
    Eagle Library   – Eagle Library
    Dodge Ltd.   – Dodge Co.
    Stromberg Carlson   – Stromberg Carlsen
    Clairice Ling   – Clairice Linng
    Mason Book Co.   – Matson Book Co.

LIST 5   5._____
    66273   – 66273
    629   – 629
    7382517283   – 7382517283
    637281   – 639281
    2738261   – 2788261

LIST 6   6._____
    Robert MacColl   – Robert McColl
    Buick Motor   – Buck Motors
    Murray Bay & Co. Ltd. – Murray Bay Co. Ltd.
    L.T. Ltyle   – L.T. Lyttle
    A.S. Landas   – A.S. Landas

2 (#2)

LIST 7　　　　　　　　　　　　　　　　　　　　　　　　　　　　　　　　　7.____
 6271526374890 – 627152637490
 73526189 – 73526189
 5372 – 5392
 637281142 – 63728124
 4783946 – 4783046

LIST 8　　　　　　　　　　　　　　　　　　　　　　　　　　　　　　　　　8.____
 Tyndall Burke – Tyndell Burke
 W. Briehl – W. Briehl
 Burritt Publishing Co. – Buritt Publishing Co.
 Frederick Breyer & Co. – Frederick Breyer Co.
 Bailey Buulard – Bailey Bullard

LIST 9　　　　　　　　　　　　　　　　　　　　　　　　　　　　　　　　　9.____
 634 – 634
 16837 – 163837
 273892223678 – 27389223678
 527182 – 527782
 3628901223 – 3629002223

LIST 10　　　　　　　　　　　　　　　　　　　　　　　　　　　　　　　　10.____
 Ernest Boas – Ernest Boas
 Rankin Barne – Rankin Barnes
 Edward Appley – Edward Appely
 Camel – Camel
 Caiger Food Co. – Caiger Food Co.

LIST 11　　　　　　　　　　　　　　　　　　　　　　　　　　　　　　　　11.____
 6273 – 6273
 322 – 332
 15672839 – 15672839
 63728192637 – 63728192639
 738 – 738

LIST 12　　　　　　　　　　　　　　　　　　　　　　　　　　　　　　　　12.____
 Wells Fargo Co. – Wells Fargo Co.
 W.D. Brett – W.D. Britt
 Tassco Co. – Tassko Co.
 Republic Mills – Republic Mill
 R.W. Burnham – R.W. Burhnam

LIST 13　　　　　　　　　　　　　　　　　　　　　　　　　　　　　　　　13.____
 7253529152 – 7283529152
 6283 – 6383
 52839102738 – 5283910238
 308 – 398
 82637201927 – 8263720127

3 (#2)

LIST 14   14.____
    Schumacker Co.   – Shumacker Co.
    C.H. Caiger   – C.H. Caiger
    Abraham Strauss   – Abram Straus
    B.F. Boettjer   – B.F. Boettijer
    Cut-Rate Store   – Cut-Rate Stores

LIST 15   15.____
    15273826   – 15273826
    72537   – 73537
    726391027384   – 62639107384
    637389   – 627399
    725382910   – 725382910

LIST 16   16.____
    Hixby Ltd.   – Hixby Lt'd.
    S. Reiner   – S. Riener
    Reynard Co.   – Reynord Co.
    Esso Gassoline Co. – Esso Gasolene Co.
    Belle Brock   – Belle Brock

LIST 17   17.____
    7245   – 7245
    819263728192   – 819263728172
    682537289   – 682537298
    789   – 789
    82936542891   – 82936542891

LIST 18   18.____
    Joseph Cartwright   – Joseph Cartwrite
    Foote Food Co.   – Foot Food Co.
    Weiman & Held   – Weiman & Held
    Sanderson Shoe Co. – Sandersen Shoe Co.
    A.M. Byrne   – A.N. Byrne

LIST 19   19.____
    4738267   – 4738277
    63728   – 63729
    6283628901   – 6283628991
    918264   – 918264
    263728192037   – 2637728192073

LIST 20   20.____
    Exray Laboratories   – Exray Labratories
    Curley Toy Co.   – Curly Toy Co.
    J. Lauer & Cross   – J. Laeur & Cross
    Mireco Brands   – Mireco Brands
    Sandor Lorand   – Sandor Larand

4 (#2)

LIST 21   21._____
    607   – 609
    6405   – 6403
    976   – 996
    101267   – 101267
    2065432   – 20965432

LIST 22   22._____
    John Macy & Sons   – John Macy & Son
    Venus Pencil Co.   – Venus Pencil Co.
    Nell McGinnis   – Nell McGinnis
    McCutcheon & Co.   – McCutcheon & Co.
    Sun-Tan Oil   – Sun-Tan Oil

LIST 23   23._____
    703345700   – 703345700
    46754   – 466754
    3367490   – 3367490
    3379   – 3778
    47384   – 47394

LIST 24   24._____
    arthritis   – arthritis
    asthma   – asthma
    endocrine   – endocrene
    gastro-enterological – gastrol-enteralogical
    orthopedic   – orthopedic

LIST 25   25._____
    743829432   – 743828432
    998   – 998
    732816253902   – 732816252902
    46829   – 46830
    7439120249   – 7439210249

KEY (CORRECT ANSWERS)

1.	4		11.	3
2.	3		12.	1
3.	2		13.	1
4.	1		14.	1
5.	2		15.	2
6.	1		16.	1
7.	2		17.	3
8.	1		18.	1
9.	1		19.	1
10.	3		20.	1

21. 1
22. 4
23. 2
24. 3
25. 1

NAME AND NUMBER CHECKING
EXAMINATION SECTION
TEST 1

DIRECTIONS: Questions 1 through 17 consist of sets of names and addresses. In each question, the name and address in Column II should be an exact copy of the name and address in Column I.
If there is:
a mistake only in the name, mark your answer A;
a mistake only in the address, mark your answer B;
a mistake in both name and address, mark your answer C;
No mistake in either name or address, mark your answer D.

Sample Question

Column I	Column II
Christina Magnusson	Christina Magnusson
288 Greene Street	288 Greene Street
New York, N.Y. 10003	New York, N.Y. 10013

Since there is a mistake only in the address (the zip code should be 10003 instead of 10013), the answer to the sample question is B.

COLUMN I	COLUMN II	
1. Ms. Joan Kelly 313 Franklin Avenue Brooklyn, N.Y. 11202	Ms. Joan Kielly 318 Franklin Ave. Brooklyn, N.Y. 11202	1.____
2. Mrs. Eileen Engel 47-24 86 Road Queens, N.Y. 11122	Mrs. Ellen Engel 47-24 86 Road Queens, New York 11122	2.____
3. Marcia Michaels 213 E. 81 St. New York, N.Y. 10012	Marcia Michaels 213 E. 81 St. New York, N.Y. 10012	3.____
4. Rev. Edward J. Smyth 1401 Brandeis Street San Francisco, Calif. 96201	Rev. Edward J. Smyth 1401 Brandies Street San Francisco, Calif. 96201	4.____
5. Alicia Rodriguez 24-68 82 St. Elmhurst, N.Y. 11122	Alicia Rodriguez 2468 81 St. Elmhurst, N.Y. 11122	5.____

2 (#1)

COLUMN I	COLUMN II	
6. Ernest Eisemann 21 Columbia St. New York, N.Y. 10007	Ernest Eisermann 21 Columbia St. New York, N.Y. 10007	6.____
7. Mr. & Mrs. George Petersson 87-11 91st Avenue Woodhaven, N.Y. 11421	Mr. & Mrs. George Peterson 87-11 91st Avenue Woodhaven, N.Y. 11421	7.____
8. Mr. Ivan Klebnikov 1848 Newkirk Avenue Brooklyn, N.Y. 11226	Mr. Ivan Klebikov 1848 Newkirk Avenue Brooklyn, N.Y. 11622	8.____
9. Mr. Samuel Rothfleisch 71 Pine Street New York, N.Y. 10005	Samuel Rothfleisch 71 Pine Street New York, N.Y. 100005	9.____
10. Mrs. Isabel Tonnessen 198 East 185th Street Bronx, N.Y. 10458	Mrs. Isabel Tonnessen 189 East 185th Street Bronx, N.Y. 10348	10.____
11. Esteban Perez 173 Eighth Street Staten Island, N.Y. 10306	Estaban Perez 173 Eighth Street Staten Island, N.Y. 10306	11.____
12. Esta Wong 141 West 68 St. New York, N.Y. 10023	Esta Wang 141 West 68 St. New York, N.Y. 10023	12.____
13. Dr. Alberto Grosso 3475 12th Avenue Brooklyn, N.Y. 11218	Dr. Alberto Grosso 3475 12th Avenue Brooklyn, N.Y. 11218	13.____
14. Mrs. Ruth Bortias 482 Theresa Ct. Far Rockaway, N.Y. 11691	Ms. Ruth Bortlas 482 Theresa Ct. Far Rockaway, N.Y. 11169	14.____
15. Mr. & Mrs. Howard Fox 2301 Sedgwick Ave. Bronx, N.Y. 10468	Mr. & Mrs. Howard Fox 231 Sedgwick Ave. Bronx, N.Y. 10468	15.____
16. Miss Marjorie Black 223 East 23 Street New York, N.Y. 10010	Miss Margorie Black 223 East 23 Street New York, N.Y. 10010	16.____

3 (#1)

COLUMN I

17. Michelle Herman
806 Valley Rd.
Old Tappan, N.J. 07675

COLUMN II

Michelle Hermann
806 Valley Dr.
Old Tappan, N.J. 07675

17._____

KEY (CORRECT ANSWERS)

1.	C	7.	A	13.	D
2.	A	8.	C	14.	C
3.	D	9.	D	15.	B
4.	B	10.	B	16.	A
5.	B	11.	A	17.	C
6.	A	12.	D		

TEST 2

DIRECTIONS: Questions 1 through 15 are to be answered SOLELY on the instructions given below. *PRINT THE LETTER OF THE CORRECT ANSWER IN THE SPACE AT THE RIGHT.*

INSTRUCTIONS

In each of the following questions, the 3-line name and address in Column I is the master-list entry, and the 3-line entry in Column II is the information to be checked against the master list. If there is one line that does not match, mark your answer A; if there are two lines that do not match, mark your answer B; if all three lines do not match, mark your answer C; if the lines all match exactly, mark your answer D.

Sample Question

Column I
Mark L. Field
11-09 Price Park Blvd.
Bronx, N.Y. 11402

Column II
Mark L. Field
11-99 Prince Park Way
Bronx, N.Y. 11401

The first lines in each column match exactly. The second lines do not match since 11-09 does not match 11-99; and Blvd. does not match Way. The third lines do not match either since 11402 does not match 11401. Therefore, there are two lines that do not match, and the CORRECT answer is B.

	COLUMN I	COLUMN II	
1.	Jerome A. Jackson 1243 14th Avenue New York, N.Y. 10023	Jerome A. Johnson 1234 14th Avenue New York, N.Y. 10023	1.____
2.	Sophie Strachtheim 33-28 Connecticut Ave. Far Rockaway, N.Y. 11697	Sophie Strachtheim 33-28 Connecticut Ave. Far Rockaway, N.Y. 11697	2.____
3.	Elisabeth N.T. Gorrell 256 Exchange St. New York, N.Y. 10013	Elizabeth N.T. Gorrell 256 Exchange St. New York, N.Y. 10013	3.____
4.	Maria J. Gonzalez 7516 E. Sheepshead Rd. Brooklyn, N.Y. 11240	Maria J. Gonzalez 7516 N. Shepshead Rd. Brooklyn, N.Y. 11240	4.____
5.	Leslie B. Brautenweiler 21 57A Seiler Terr. Flushing, N.Y. 11367	Leslie B. Brautenwieler 21-75A Seiler Terr. Flushing, N.J. 11367	5.____

2 (#2)

COLUMN I	COLUMN II	
6. Rigoberto J. Peredes 157 Twin Towers, #18F Tottenville, S. I., N.Y,	Rigoberto J. Peredes 157 Twin Towers, #18F Tottenville, S.I., N.Y.	6.____
7. Pietro F. Albino P.O. Box 7548 Floral Park, N.Y. 11005	Pietro F. Albina P.O. Box 7458 Floral Park, N.Y. 11005	7.____
8. Joanne Zimmerman Bldg. SW, Room 314 532-4601	Joanne Zimmermann Bldg. SW, Room 314 532-4601	8.____
9. Carlyle Whetstone Payroll Div. –A, Room 212A 262-5000, ext. 471	Carlyle Whetstone Payroll Div. –A, Room 212A 262-5000, ext. 417	9.____
10. Kenneth Chiang Legal Council, Room 9745 (201) 416-9100, ext. 17	Kenneth Chiang Legal Counsel, Room 9745 (201) 416-9100, Ext. 17	10.____
11. Ethel Koenig Personnel Services Division, Room 433; 635-7572	Ethel Hoenig Personal Services Division, Room 433; 635-7527	11.____
12. Joyce Ehrhardt Office of the Administrator, Room W56; 387-8706	Joyce Ehrhart Office of the Administrator, Room W56; 387-7806	12.____
13. Ruth Lang EAM Bldg., Room C101 625-2000, ext. 765	Ruth Lang EAM Bldg., Room C110 625-2000, ext. 765	13.____
14. Anne Marie Ionozzi Investigations, Room 827 576-4000, ext. 832	Anna Marie Ionozzi Investigation, Room 827 566-4000, ext. 832	14.____
15. Willard Jameson Fm C Bldg., Room 687 454-3010	Willard Jamieson Fm C Bldg., Room 687 454-3010	15.____

KEY (CORRECT ANSWERS)

1. B
2. D
3. A
4. A
5. C
6. D
7. B
8. D
9. B
10. A
11. C
12. B
13. A
14. C
15. A

TEST 3

DIRECTIONS: Questions 1 through 10 are to be answered on the basis of the following instructions. *PRINT THE LETTER OF THE CORRECT ANSWER IN THE SPACE AT THE RIGHT.*

INSTRUCTIONS

For each such set of names, addresses, and numbers listed in Columns I and II, select your answer from the following options:
- The names in Columns I and II are different,
- The addresses in Columns I and II are different,
- The numbers in Columns I and II are different,
- The names, addresses, and numbers in Columns I and II are identical.

	COLUMN I	COLUMN II	
1.	Francis Jones 62 Stately Avenue 96-12446	Francis Jones 62 Stately Avenue 96-21446	1.____
2.	Julio Montez 19 Ponderosa Road 56-73161	Julio Montez 19 Ponderosa Road 56-71361	2.____
3.	Mary Mitchell 2314 Melbourne Drive 68-92172	Mary Mitchell 2314 Melbourne Drive 68-92172	3.____
4.	Harry Patterson 25 Dunne Street 14-33430	Harry Patterson 25 Dunne Street 14-34330	4.____
5.	Patrick Murphy 171 West Hosmer Street 93-81214	Patrick Murphy 171 West Hosmer Street 93-18214	5.____
6.	August Schultz 816 St. Clair Avenue 53-40149	August Schultz 816 St. Claire Avenue 53-40149	6.____
7.	George Taft 72 Runnymede Street 47-04033	George Taft 72 Runnymede Street 47-04023	7.____
8.	Angus Henderson 1418 Madison Street 81-76375	Angus Henderson 1318 Madison Street 81-76375	8.____

COLUMN I	COLUMN II	
9. Carolyn Mazur 12 Riverview Road 38-99615	Carolyn Mazur 12 Rivervane Road 38-99615	9.____
10. Adele Russell 1725 Lansing Lane 72-91962	Adela Russell 1725 Lansing Lane 72-91962	10.____

KEY (CORRECT ANSWERS)

1.	C	6.	B
2.	C	7.	C
3.	D	8.	D
4.	C	9.	B
5.	C	10.	A

TEST 4

DIRECTIONS: Questions 1 through 20 test how good you are at catching mistakes in typing or printing. In each question, the name and address in Column II should be an exact copy of the name and address in Column I. Mark your answer
  A. If there is no mistake in either name or address;
  B. If there is a mistake in both name and address;
  C. If there is a mistake only in the name;
  D. If there is a mistake only in the address.
PRINT THE LETTER OF THE CORRECT ANSWER IN THE SPACE AT THE RIGHT.

COLUMN I | COLUMN II

1. Milos Yanocek
    33-60 14 Street
    Long Island City, N.Y. 11011

    Milos Yanocek
    33-60 14 Street
    Long Island City, N.Y. 11001   1.____

2. Alphonse Sabattelo
    24 Minnetta Lane
    New York, N.Y. 10006

    Alphonse Sabbattelo
    24 Minetta Lane
    New York, N.Y. 10006   2.____

3. Helen Steam
    5 Metropolitan Oval
    Bronx, N.Y. 10462

    Helene Stearn
    5 Metropolitan Oval
    Bronx, N.Y. 10462   3.____

4. Jacob Weisman
    231 Francis Lewis Boulevard
    Forest Hills, N.Y. 11325

    Jacob Weisman
    231 Francis Lewis Boulevard
    Forest Hills, N.Y. 11325   4.____

5. Riccardo Fuente
    134 West 83 Street
    New York, N.Y. 10024

    Riccardo Fuentes
    134 West 88 Street
    New York, N.Y. 10024   5.____

6. Dennis Lauber
    52 Avenue D
    Brooklyn, N.Y. 11216

    Dennis Lauder
    52 Avenue D
    Brooklyn, N.Y. 11216   6.____

7. Paul Cutter
    195 Galloway Avenue
    Staten Island, N.Y. 10356

    Paul Cutter
    175 Galloway Avenue
    Staten Island, N.Y. 10365   7.____

8. Sean Donnelly
    45-58 41 Avenue
    Woodside, N.Y. 11168

    Sean Donnelly
    45-58 41 Avenue
    Woodside, N.Y. 11168   8.____

9. Clyde Willot
    1483 Rockaway Avenue
    Brooklyn, N.Y. 11238

    Clyde Willat
    1483 Rockaway Avenue
    Brooklyn, N.Y. 11238   9.____

2 (#4)

COLUMN I	COLUMN II	
10. Michael Stanakis 419 Sheriden Avenue Staten Island, N.Y. 10363	Michael Stanakis 419 Sheraden Avenue Staten Island, N.Y. 10363	10.____
11. Joseph DiSilva 63-84 Saunders Road Rego Park, N.Y. 11431	Joseph Disilva 64-83 Saunders Road Rego Park, N.Y. 11431	11.____
12. Linda Polansky 2224 Fendon Avenue Bronx, N.Y. 20464	Linda Polansky 2255 Fenton Avenue Bronx, N.Y. 10464	12.____
13. Alfred Klein 260 Hillside Terrace Staten Island, N.Y. 15545	Alfred Klein 260 Hillside Terrace Staten Island, N.Y. 15545	13.____
14. William McDonnell 504 E. 55 Street New York, N.Y. 10103	William McConnell 504 E. 55 Street New York, N.Y. 10108	14.____
15. Angela Cipolla 41-11 Parson Avenue Flushing, N.Y. 11446	Angela Cipola 41-11 Parsons Avenue Flushing, N.Y. 11446	15.____
16. Julie Sheridan 1212 Ocean Avenue Brooklyn, N.Y. 11237	Julia Sheridan 1212 Ocean Avenue Brooklyn, N.Y. 11237	16.____
17. Arturo Rodriguez 2156 Cruger Avenue Bronx, N.Y. 10446	Arturo Rodrigues 2156 Cruger Avenue Bronx, N.Y. 10446	17.____
18. Helen McCabe 2044 East 19 Street Brooklyn, N.Y. 11204	Helen McCabe 2040 East 19 Street Brooklyn, N.Y. 11204	18.____
19. Charles Martin 526 West 160 Street New York, N.Y. 10022	Charles Martin 526 West 160 Street New York, N.Y. 10022	19.____
20. Morris Rabinowitz 31 Avenue M Brooklyn, N.Y. 11216	Morris Rabinowitz 31 Avenue N Brooklyn, N.Y. 11216	20.____

KEY (CORRECT ANSWERS)

1.	D	11.	B
2.	B	12.	D
3.	C	13.	A
4.	A	14.	B
5.	B	15.	B
6.	C	16.	C
7.	D	17.	C
8.	A	18.	D
9.	B	19.	A
10.	D	20.	D

TEST 5

DIRECTIONS: In copying the addresses below from Column A to the same line in Column B, an Agent-in-Training made some errors. For Questions 1 through 5, if you find that the agent made an error in
only one line, mark your answer A;
only two lines, mark your answer B;
only three lines, mark your answer C;
all four lines, mark your answer D.

EXAMPLE

COLUMN A	COLUMN B
24 Third Avenue	24 Third Avenue
5 Lincoln Road	5 Lincoln Street
50 Central Park West	6 Central Park West
37-21 Queens Boulevard	21-37 Queens Boulevard

Since errors were made on only three lines, namely the second, third, and fourth, the CORRECT answer is C.
PRINT THE LETTER OF THE CORRECT ANSWER IN THE SPACE AT THE RIGHT.

COLUMN A   COLUMN B

1. 57-22 Springfield Boulevard   75-22 Springfield Boulevard   1.____
   94 Gun Hill Road   94 Gun Hill Avenue
   8 New Dorp Lane   8 New Drop Lane
   36 Bedford Avenue   36 Bedford Avenue

2. 538 Castle Hill Avenue   538 Castle Hill Avenue   2.____
   54-15 Beach Channel Drive   54-15 Beach Channel Drive
   21 Ralph Avenue   21 Ralph Avenue
   162 Madison Avenue   162 Morrison Avenue

3. 49 Thomas Street   49 Thomas Street   3.____
   27-21 Northern Blvd.   21-27 Northern Blvd.
   86 125th Street   86 125th Street
   872 Atlantic Ave.   872 Baltic Ave,

4. 261-17 Horace Harding Expwy.   261-17 Horace Harding Pkwy.   4.____
   191 Fordham Road   191 Fordham Road
   6 Victory Blvd.   6 Victoria Blvd.
   552 Oceanic Ave.   552 Ocean Ave.

5. 90-05 38th Avenue   90-05 36th Avenue   5.____
   19 Central Park West   19 Central Park East
   9281 Avenue X   9281 Avenue X
   22 West Farms Square   22 West Farms Square

KEY (CORRECT ANSWERS)

1. C
2. A
3. B
4. C
5. B

TEST 6

DIRECTIONS: For Questions 1 through 10, choose the letter in Column II next to the number which EXACTLY matches the number in Column I. *PRINT THE LETTER OF THE CORRECT ANSWER IN THE SPACE AT THE RIGHT.*

COLUMN I & COLUMN II

1. 14235
   A. 13254
   B. 12435
   C. 13245
   D. 14235

   1.____

2. 70698
   A. 90768
   B. 60978
   C. 70698]
   D. 70968

   2.____

3. 11698
   A. 11689
   B. 11986
   C. 11968
   D. 11698

   3.____

4. 50497
   A. 50947
   B. 50497
   C. 50749
   D. 54097

   4.____

5. 69635
   A. 60653
   B. 69630
   C. 69365
   D. 69635

   5.____

6. 1201022011
   A. 1201022011
   B. 1201020211
   C. 1202012011
   D. 1021202011

   6.____

7. 3893981389
   A. 3893891389
   B. 3983981389
   C. 3983891389
   D. 3893981389

   7.____

8. 4765476589
   A. 4765476598
   B. 4765476588
   C. 4765476589
   D. 4765746589

   8.____

9. 8679678938
    A. 8679687938
    B. 8679678938
    C. 8697678938
    D. 8678678938

    9.____

10. 6834836932
    A. 6834386932
    B. 6834836923
    C. 6843836932
    D. 6834836932

    10.____

Questions 11-15.

DIRECTIONS: For Questions 11 through 15, determine how many of the symbols in Column Z are exactly the same as the symbol in Column Y.
If none is exactly the same, answer A;
If only one symbol is exactly the same, answer B;
If two symbols are exactly the same, answer C;
If three symbols are exactly the same, answer D.

COLUMN Y	COLUMN Z	
11. A123B1266	A123B1366 A123B1266 A133B1366 A123B1266	11.____
12. CC28D3377	CD22D3377 CC38D3377 CC28C3377 CC28D2277	12.____
13. M21AB201X	M12AB201X M21AB201X M21AB201Y M21BA201X	13.____
14. PA383Y744	AP383Y744 PA338Y744 PA388Y744 PA383Y774	14.____
15. PB2Y8893	PB2Y8893 PB2Y8893 PB3Y8898 PB2Y8893	15.____

KEY (CORRECT ANSWERS)

1.	D	6.	A	11.	C
2.	C	7.	D	12.	A
3.	D	8.	C	13.	B
4.	B	9.	B	14.	A
5.	D	10.	D	15.	D

WORD MEANING
EXAMINATION SECTION
TEST 1

DIRECTIONS: For the following questions, select the word or group of words lettered A, B, C, D, or E that means MOST NEARLY the same as the word in capital letters. *PRINT THE LETTER OF THE CORRECT ANSWER IN THE SPACE AT THE RIGHT.*

1. The directors plan to EXPAND the factory. 1.____
   A. shut down   B. remodel   C. enlarge   D. erect   E. occupy

2. The CAPTIVE pleaded for mercy. 2.____
   A. savage   B. spy   C. jailer   D. officer   E. prisoner

3. The policeman CONSOLED the weeping child. 3.____
   A. found   B. carried home   C. scolded
   D. comforted   E. played with

4. On these slopes there is very little VEGETATION. 4.____
   A. traffic   B. rocky soil   C. plant life
   D. moisture   E. bird life

5. The pupil was criticized for his SLIPSHOD work. 5.____
   A. slow   B. childish   C. uncompleted
   D. careless   E. incorrect

6. The names of characters in plays are usually FICTITIOUS. 6.____
   A. odd   B. imaginary   C. pleasant-sounding
   D. easy to remember E. well-known

7. The most interesting part of the book was the PREFACE. 7.____
   A. title page   B. introduction   C. table of contents
   D. cover design   E. illustrations

8. The bullet PENETRATED the wall. 8.____
   A. entered into   B. dented   C. bounded off
   D. passed over   E. weakened

9. The large mustache made the actor look VILLAINOUS. 9.____
   A. dignified   B. slightly older   C. very wicked
   D. untidy   E. uncomfortable

10. They hoped to EXTERMINATE the insects. 10.____
    A. destroy   B. collect   C. classify
    D. experiment with E. drive away

113

11. It is my CONVICTION that you are wrong.

    A. fear B. fault C. firm belief D. imagination E. recollection

12. A good employee is always PUNCTUAL.

    A. polite B. neat C. thoughtful D. prompt E. truthful

13. The actor played a JUVENILE role.

    A. lovesick B. humorous C. criminal D. modern E. youthful

14. In business letters we state our business CONCISELY.

    A. accurately B. fully C. briefly D. politely E. officially

15. We found that the goods on sale were of INFERIOR quality.

    A. second-rate B. excellent C. lasting
    D. noticeable E. surprising

KEY (CORRECT ANSWERS)

1. C
2. E
3. D
4. C
5. D
6. B
7. B
8. A
9. C
10. A
11. C
12. D
13. E
14. C
15. A

TEST 2

DIRECTIONS: For the following questions, select the word or group of words lettered A, B, C, D, or E that means MOST NEARLY the same as the word in capital letters. *PRINT THE LETTER OF THE CORRECT ANSWER IN THE SPACE AT THE RIGHT.*

1. The sword has a KEEN edge.

   A. bright   B. sharp   C. steel   D. polished   E. rough

2. He STARTLED the boy who was trying to unlock the car.

   A. surprised   B. punished   C. chased   D. arrested   E. helped

3. FORTHCOMING events were listed on the club bulletin board.

   A. weekly   B. interesting   C. outstanding
   D. social   E. approaching

4. The lawyer's next question ASTOUNDED the witness.

   A. misled   B. amazed   C. depressed   D. pleased   E. angered

5. In his hand the hiker was carrying a large STAFF.

   A. pack   B. loaf   C. stick
   D. musical instrument   E. garment

6. We nervously awaited the doctor's VERDICT.

   A. arrival   B. call   C. approval
   D. decision   E. prescription

7. The hikers noticed several CREVICES in the rocks.

   A. plants   B. uneven spots   C. fossils
   D. water holes   E. cracks

8. Such training helps to make a boy SELF-SUFFICIENT.

   A. clever   B. healthy   C. conceited
   D. independent   E. uncomfortable

9. The door was left AJAR.

   A. slightly opened   B. unhinged   C. unguarded
   D. unlocked   E. completely blocked

10. They talked about INSIGNIFICANT matters.

    A. unimportant   B. thrilling   C. puzzling
    D. unpleasant   E. secret

11. The child was given a good mark for DEPORTMENT. 11.___

    A. intelligence B. attendance C. health D. behavior E. neatness

12. Because of PRIOR engagements, she refused the invitation. 12.___

    A. personal   B. more urgent   C. more attractive
    D. future   E. earlier

13. The delegates will CONVENE at noon. 13.___

    A. dine   B. vote   C. debate   D. assemble   E. agree

14. Modern methods bring more REVENUE to the farmer. 14.___

    A. taxes   B. income   C. produce   D. leisure   E. acreage

15. The machine has MANUAL controls. 15.___

    A. self-acting   B. double   C. hand-operated
    D. simple   E. handmade

KEY (CORRECT ANSWERS)

1. B	6. D
2. A	7. E
3. E	8. D
4. B	9. A
5. C	10. A

11. D
12. E
13. D
14. B
15. C

TEST 3

DIRECTIONS: For the following questions, select the word or group of words lettered A, B, C, D, or E that means MOST NEARLY the same as the word in capital letters. *PRINT THE LETTER OF THE CORRECT ANSWER IN THE SPACE AT THE RIGHT.*

1. Grandfather ACQUIRED ten acres of pasture land.

    A. obtained   B. plowed   C. sold   D. leased   E. desired

2. A feeling of EXHAUSTION came over the players during the game.

    A. fear   B. extreme tiredness   C. overconfidence
    D. unsteadiness   E. complete happiness

3. We pitied the child in the GRIMY clothes.

    A. ill-fitting   B. secondhand   C. poorly made
    D. dirty   E. ragged

4. The mechanic's calculations were APPROXIMATE.

    A. nearly exact   B. remarkable   C. hastily made
    D. worthless   E. mathematically correct

5. A COMPETENT young woman was given the position.

    A. busy   B. pretty   C. capable
    D. friendly   E. good-natured

6. We had BARELY finished by six o'clock.

    A. easily   B. only just   C. partly
    D. more or less   E. unexpectedly

7. His second offense was more GRIEVOUS than his first. GRIEVOUS means *most nearly*

    A. serious   B. stupid   C. deliberate   D. excusable   E. peculiar

8. All air traffic was SUSPENDED during the emergency.

    A. turned back   B. speeded up   C. stopped
    D. relieved   E. repaired

9. The antics of the monkeys DIVERTED the children.

    A. upset   B. amused   C. surprised   D. disgusted   E. frightened

10. The man SURVIVED his three sisters.

    A. loved   B. envied   C. outlived   D. destroyed   E. excelled

11. Franklin was a man of EXCEPTIONAL ability.

    A. well-trained B. active C. mechanical
    D. self-educated E. unusual

12. Their aim seems to be to THWART our plans.

    A. simplify B. direct C. rely on
    D. block E. keep up with

13. He heard the warning cry of another PEDESTRIAN.

    A. agent B. walker C. passenger
    D. workingman E. traffic officer

14. They boasted about the SUPERIORITY of their product.

    A. beauty B. abundance C. excellence
    D. popularity E. permanence

15. We considered their point of view ABSURD.

    A. disgusting B. old-fashioned C. insincere
    D. reasonable E. foolish

KEY (CORRECT ANSWERS)

1. A
2. B
3. D
4. A
5. C

6. B
7. A
8. C
9. B
10. C

11. E
12. D
13. B
14. C
15. E

TEST 4

DIRECTIONS: For the following questions, select the word or group of words lettered A, B, C, D, or E that means MOST NEARLY the same as the word in capital letters. *PRINT THE LETTER OF THE CORRECT ANSWER IN THE SPACE AT THE RIGHT.*

1. Our neighbor PURCHASED his home last year. 1._____
   A. bought   B. rented   C. painted   D. remodeled   E. built

2. The only sound was the STEADY ticking of the clock. 2._____
   A. noisy   B. rapid   C. regular   D. cheerful   E. tiresome

3. The desks in our room are STATIONARY. 3._____
   A. heavy   B. not movable   C. metal
   D. easily adjustable   E. standard

4. Before signing the papers, Mr. Edmond consulted his ATTORNEY. 4._____
   A. banker   B. clerk   C. lawyer   D. secretary   E. employer

5. We IMITATE those whom we admire. 5._____
   A. protect   B. attract   C. study   D. copy   E. appreciate

6. They reached the SUMMIT of the mountain by noon. 6._____
   A. base   B. wooded area   C. side
   D. face   E. top

7. The motorist HEEDED the signals. 7._____
   A. worried about   B. passed by   C. took notice of
   D. laughed at   E. disagreed with

8. The SEVERITY of their criticism upset us. 8._____
   A. purpose   B. harshness   C. method
   D. suddenness   E. unfairness

9. We made a very LEISURELY trip to California. 9._____
   A. roundabout   B. unhurried   C. unforgettable
   D. tiresome   E. speedy

10. The little girl shook her head VIGOROUSLY. 10._____
    A. sadly   B. hopefully   C. sleepily
    D. thoughtfully   E. energetically

KEYS (CORRECT ANSWERS)

1. A
2. C
3. B
4. C
5. D

6. E
7. C
8. B
9. B
10. E

READING COMPREHENSION
UNDERSTANDING AND INTERPRETING WRITTEN MATERIAL
EXAMINATION SECTION
TEST 1

DIRECTIONS: The following questions are intended to test your ability to read with comprehension and to understand and interpret written materials, particularly legal passages. It will be necessary for you to read each paragraph carefully because the questions are based only on the material contained therein.
Each question has several suggested answers. *PRINT THE LETTER OF THE CORRECT ANSWER IN THE SPACE AT THE RIGHT.*

Questions 1-3.

DIRECTIONS: Answer Questions 1 to 3 *SOLELY* on the basis of the following statement:

Foot patrol has some advantages over all other methods of patrol. Maximum opportunity is provided for observation within range of the senses and for close contact with people and things that enable the patrolman to provide a maximum service as an information source and counselor to the public and as the eyes and ears of the police department. A foot patrolman loses no time in alighting from a vehicle, and the performance of police tasks is not hampered by responsibility for his vehicle while afoot. Foot patrol, however, does not have many of the advantages of a patrol car. Lack of both mobility and immediate communication with headquarters lessens the officer's value in an emergency. The area that he can cover effectively is limited and, therefore, this method of patrol is costly.

1. According to this paragraph, the foot patrolman is the eyes and ears of the police department because he is

   A. in direct contact with the station house
   B. not responsible for a patrol vehicle
   C. able to observe closely conditions on his patrol post
   D. a readily available information source to the public

2. The *MOST* accurate of the following statements concerning the various methods of patrol, according to this paragraph, is that

   A. foot patrol should sometimes be combined with motor patrol
   B. foot patrol is better than motor patrol
   C. helicopter patrol has the same advantages as motor patrol
   D. motor patrol is more readily able to communicate with superior officers in an emergency

3. According to this paragraph, it is *CORRECT* to state that foot patrol is

   A. *economical* since increased mobility makes more rapid action possible
   B. *expensive* since the area that can be patrolled is relatively small
   C. *economical* since vehicle costs need not be considered
   D. *expensive* since giving information to the public is time-consuming

Questions 4-6.

DIRECTIONS: Answer Questions 4 to 6 SOLELY on the basis of the following statement:
All applicants for an original license to operate a catering establishment shall be fingerprinted. This shall include the officers, employees, and stockholders of the company and the members of a partnership. In case of a change, by addition or substitution, occurring during the existence of a license, the person added or substituted shall be fingerprinted. However, in the case of a hotel containing more than 200 rooms, only the officer or manager filing the application is required to be fingerprinted. The police commissioner may also at his discretion exempt the employees and stockholders of any company. The fingerprints shall be taken on one copy of form C.E. 20 and on two copies of C.E. 21. One copy of form C.E. 21 shall accompany the application. Fingerprints are not required with a renewal application.

4. According to this paragraph, an employee added to the payroll of a licensed catering establishment which is not in a hotel, must

   A. always be fingerprinted
   B. be fingerprinted unless he has been previously fingerprinted for another license
   C. be fingerprinted unless exempted by the police commissioner
   D. be fingerprinted only if he is the manager or an officer of the company

5. According to this paragraph, it would be MOST accurate to state that

   A. form C.E. 20 must accompany a renewal application
   B. form C.E. 21 must accompany all applications
   C. form C.E. 21 must accompany an original application
   D. both forms C.E. 20 and C.E. 21 must accompany all applications

6. A hotel of 270 rooms has applied for a license to operate a catering establishment on the premises. According to the instructions for fingerprinting given in this paragraph, the

   A. officers, employees, and stockholders shall be fingerprinted
   B. officers and manager shall be fingerprinted
   C. employees shall be fingerprinted
   D. officer filing the application shall be fingerprinted

Questions 7-9.

DIRECTIONS: Answer Questions 7 to 9 SOLELY on the basis of the following statement:
It is difficult to instill in young people inner controls on aggressive behavior in a world marked by aggression. The slum child's environment, full of hostility, stimulates him to delinquency; he does that which he sees about him. The time to act against delinquency is before it is committed. It is clear that juvenile delinquency, especially when it is committed in groups or gangs, leads almost inevitably to an adult criminal life unless it is checked at once. The first signs of vandalism and disregard for the comfort, health, and property of the community should be considered as storm warnings which cannot be ignored. The delinquent's first crime has the underlying element of testing the law and its ability to hit back.

7. A *suitable* title for this entire paragraph based on the material it contains is: 7.____

   A. The Need for Early Prevention of Juvenile Delinquency
   B. Juvenile Delinquency as a Cause of Slums
   C. How Aggressive Behavior Prevents Juvenile Delinquency
   D. The Role of Gangs in Crime

8. According to this paragraph, an *INITIAL* act of juvenile crime *usually* involves a(n) 8.____

   A. group or gang activity
   B. theft of valuable property
   C. test of the strength of legal authority
   D. act of physical violence

9. According to this paragraph, acts of juvenile delinquency are *most likely* to lead to a criminal career when they are 9.____

   A. acts of vandalism
   B. carried out by groups or gangs
   C. committed in a slum environment
   D. such as to impair the health of the neighborhood

Questions 10-12.

DIRECTIONS: Answer Questions 10 to 12 *SOLELY* on the basis of the following statement:
   The police laboratory performs a valuable service in crime investigation by assisting in the reconstruction of criminal action and by aiding in the identification of persons and things. When studied by a technician, physical things found at crime scenes often reveal facts useful in identifying the criminal and in determining what has occurred. The nature of substances to be examined and the character of the examinations to be made vary so widely that the services of a large variety of skilled scientific persons are needed in crime investigations. To employ such a complete staff and to provide them with equipment and standards needed for all possible analyses and comparisons is beyond the means and the needs of any but the largest police departments. The search of crime scenes for physical evidence also calls for the services of specialists supplied with essential equipment and assigned to each tour of duty so as to provide service at any hour.

10. If a police department employs a large staff of technicians of various types in its laboratory, it will affect crime investigation to the extent that 10.____

    A. most crimes will be speedily solved
    B. identification of criminals will be aided
    C. search of crime scenes for physical evidence will become of less importance
    D. investigation by police officers will not usually be required

11. According to this paragraph, the *MOST* complete study of objects found at the scenes of crimes is 11.____

    A. always done in all large police departments
    B. based on assigning one technician to each tour of duty
    C. probably done only in large police departments
    D. probably done in police departments of communities with low crime rates

12. According to this paragraph, a large variety of skilled technicians is useful in criminal investigations because   12.____

    A. crimes cannot be solved without their assistance as a part of the police team
    B. large police departments need large staffs
    C. many different kinds of tests on various substances can be made
    D. the police cannot predict what methods may be tried by wily criminals

Questions 13-14.

DIRECTIONS: Answer Questions 13 and 14 *SOLELY* on the basis of the following statement:
The emotionally unstable person is always potentially a dangerous criminal, who causes untold misery to other persons and is a source of considerable trouble and annoyance to law enforcement officials. Like his fellow criminals he will be a menace to society as long as he is permitted to be at large. Police activities against him serve to sharpen his wits, and imprisonment gives him the opportunity to learn from others how to commit more serious crimes when he is released. This criminal's mental structure makes it impossible for him to profit by his experience with the police officials, by punishment of any kind or by sympathetic understanding and treatment by well-intentioned persons, professional and otherwise.

13. According to the above paragraph, the *MOST* accurate of the following statements concerning the relationship between emotional instability and crime is that   13.____

    A. emotional instability is proof of criminal activities
    B. the emotionally unstable person can become a criminal
    C. all dangerous criminals are emotionally unstable
    D. sympathetic understanding will prevent the emotionally unstable person from becoming a criminal

14. According to the above paragraph, the effect of police activities on the emotionally unstable criminal is that   14.____

    A. police activities aid this type of criminal to reform
    B. imprisonment tends to deter this type of criminal from committing future crimes
    C. contact with the police serves to assist sympathetic understanding and medical treatment
    D. police methods against this type of criminal develop him for further unlawful acts

Questions 15-17.

DIRECTIONS: Answer Questions 15 to 17 *SOLELY* on the basis of the following statement:
Proposals to license gambling operations are based on the belief that the human desire to gamble cannot be suppressed and, therefore, it should be licensed and legalized with the people sharing in the profits, instead of allowing the underworld to benefit. If these proposals are sincere, then it is clear that only one is worthwhile at all. Legalized gambling should be completely controlled and operated by the state with all the profits used for its citizens. A state agency should be set up to operate and control the gambling business. It should be as completely removed from politics as possible. In view of the inherent nature of the gambling business, with its close relationship to lawlessness and crime, only a man of the highest integrity should be eligible to become head of this agency. However, state gambling would encourage mass gambling with its attending social and economic evils in the same manner as other forms of legal gambling; but there is no justification whatever for the business of gambling to be legalized and then permitted to operate for private profit or for the benefit of any political organization.

15. The *CENTRAL* thought of this paragraph may be *correctly* expressed as the   15.____

    A. need to legalize gambling in the state
    B. state operation of gambling for the benefit of the people
    C. need to license private gambling establishments
    D. evils of gambling

16. According to this paragraph, a problem of legalized gambling which will *still* occur if the state operates the gambling business is   16.____

    A. the diversion of profits from gambling to private use
    B. that the amount of gambling will tend to diminish
    C. the evil effects of any form of mass gambling
    D. the use of gambling revenues for illegal purposes

17. According to this paragraph, to legalize the business of gambling would be   17.____

    A. *justified* because gambling would be operated only by a man of the highest integrity
    B. *justified* because this would eliminate politics
    C. *unjustified* under any conditions because the human desire to gamble cannot be suppressed
    D. *unjustified* if operated for private or political profit

Questions 18-20.

DIRECTIONS: Answer Questions 18 to 20 *SOLELY* on the basis of the following statement:
Whenever, in the course of the performance of their duties in an emergency, members of the force operate the emergency power switch at any location on the transit system and thereby remove power from portions of the track, or they are on the scene where this has been done, they will bear in mind that, although power is removed, further dangers exist; namely, that a train may coast into the area even though the power is off, or that the rails may be energized by a train which may be in a position to transfer electricity from a live portion of the third rail through its shoe beams. Employees must look in each direction before stepping upon, crossing, or standing close to tracks, being particularly careful not to come into contact with the third rail.

18. According to this paragraph, whenever an emergency occurs which has resulted in operating the emergency power switch, it is *MOST* accurate to state that   18.____

    A. power is shut off and employees may perform their duties in complete safety
    B. there may still be power in a portion of the third rail
    C. the switch will not operate if a portion of the track has been broken
    D. trains are not permitted to stop in the area of the emergency

19. An *important* precaution which this paragraph urges employees to follow after operating the emergency power switch, is to   19.____

    A. look carefully in both directions before stepping near the rails
    B. inspect the nearest train which has stopped to see if the power is on
    C. examine the third rail to see if the power is on
    D. check the emergency power switch to make sure it has operated properly

20. A trackman reports to you, a patrolman, that a dead body is lying on the road bed. You operate the emergency power switch. A train which has been approaching comes to a stop near the scene.
   In order to act in accordance with the instructions in the above paragraph, you *should*

   A. climb down to the road bed and remove the body
   B. direct the train motorman to back up to the point where his train will not be in position to transfer electricity through its shoe beams
   C. carefully cross over the road bed to the body, avoiding the third rail and watching for train movements
   D. have the train motorman check to see if power is on before crossing to the tracks

21. The treatment to be given the offender cannot alter the fact of his offense; but we can take measures to reduce the chances of similar acts in the future. We should banish the criminal, not in order to exact revenge nor directly to encourage reform, but to deter him and others from further illegal attacks on society.
   According to this paragraph, the *PRINCIPAL* reason for punishing criminals is to

   A. prevent the commission of future crimes
   B. remove them from society
   C. avenge society
   D. teach them that crime does not pay

22. Even the most comprehensive and best substantiated summaries of the total volume of criminal acts would not contribute greatly to an understanding of the varied social and biological factors which are sometimes assumed to enter into crime causation, nor would they indicate with any degree of precision the needs of police forces in combating crime.
   According to this statement,

   A. crime statistics alone do not determine the needs of police forces in combating crime
   B. crime statistics are essential to a proper understanding of the social factors of crime
   C. social and biological factors which enter into crime causation have little bearing on police needs
   D. a knowledge of the social and biological factors of crime is essential to a proper understanding of crime statistics

23. The policeman's art consists of applying and enforcing a multitude of laws and ordinances in such degree or proportion and in such manner that the greatest degree of social protection will be secured. The degree of enforcement and the method of application will vary with each neighborhood and community.
   According to the foregoing paragraph,

   A. each neighborhood or community must judge for itself to what extent the law is to be enforced
   B. a policeman should only enforce those laws which are designed to give the greatest degree of social protection
   C. the manner and intensity of law enforcement is not necessarily the same in all communities
   D. all laws and ordinances must be enforced in a community with the same degree of intensity

24. Police control in the sense of regulating the details of police operations, involves such matters as the technical means for so organizing the available personnel that competent police leadership, when secured, can operate effectively. It is concerned not so much with the extent to which popular controls can be trusted to guide and direct the course of police protection as with the administrative relationships which should exist between the component parts of the polie organism. According to the foregoing statement, police control is

24._____

   A. solely a matter of proper personnel assignment
   B. the means employed to guide and direct the course of police protection
   C. principally concerned with the administrative relationships between units of a police organization
   D. the sum total of means employed in rendering police protection

25. Police Department Rule 5 states that a Deputy Commissioner acting as Police Commissioner shall carry out the orders of the Police Commissioner, previously given, and such orders shall not, except in cases of extreme emergency, be countermanded. This means, most nearly, that, except in cases of extreme emergency,

25._____

   A. the orders given by a Deputy Commissioner acting as Police Commissioner may not be revoked
   B. a Deputy Commissioner acting as Police Commissioner should not revoke orders previously given by the Police Commissioner
   C. a Deputy Commissioner acting as Police Commissioner is vested with the same authority to issue orders as the Police Commissioner himself
   D. only a Deputy Commissioner acting as Police Commissioner may issue orders in the absence of the Police Commissioner himself

KEY (CORRECT ANSWERS)

1.	C	11.	C
2.	D	12.	C
3.	B	13.	B
4.	C	14.	D
5.	C	15.	B
6.	D	16.	C
7.	A	17.	D
8.	C	18.	B
9.	B	19.	A
10.	B	20.	C

21.	A
22.	A
23.	C
24.	C
25.	B

TEST 2

Questions 1-2.

DIRECTIONS: Answer Questions 1 and 2 SOLELY on the basis of the following statement:
The medical examiner may contribute valuable data to the investigator of fires which cause fatalities. By careful examination of the bodies of any victims, he not only establishes cause of death, but may also furnish, in many instances, answers to questions relating to the identity of the victim and the source and origin of the fire. The medical examiner is of greatest value to law enforcement agencies because he is able to determine the exact cause of death through an examination of tissue of apparent arson victims. Thorough study of a burned body or even of parts of a burned body will frequently yield information which illuminates the problems confronting the arson investigator and the police.

1. According to the above paragraph, the MOST important task of the medical examiner in the investigation of arson is to obtain information concerning the

    A. identity of arsonists
    B. cause of death
    C. identity of victims
    D. source and origin of fires

2. The CENTRAL thought of the above paragraph is that the medical examiner aids in the solution of crimes of arson when

    A. a person is burnt to death
    B. identity of the arsonist is unknown
    C. the cause of the fire is known
    D. trained investigators are not available

Questions 3-6.

DIRECTIONS: Answer Questions 3 to 6 SOLELY on the basis of the following statement:
A foundling is an abandoned child whose identity is unknown. Desk officers shall direct the delivery, by a policewoman, if available, of foundlings actually or apparently under two years of age, to the Foundling Hospital, or if actually or apparently two years of age or over, to the Children's Center. In all other cases of dependent or neglected children, other than foundlings, requiring shelter, desk officers shall provide for obtaining such shelter as follows: between 9 a.m. and 5 p.m., Monday through Friday, by telephone direct to the Bureau of Child Welfare, in order to ascertain the shelter to which the child shall be sent; at all other times, direct the delivery of a child actually or apparently under two years of age to the Foundling Hospital, or, if the child is actually or apparently two years of age or over, to the Children's Center.

3. According to this paragraph, it would be MOST correct to state that

    A. a foundling as well as a neglected child may be delivered to the Foundling Hospital
    B. a foundling but not a neglected child may be delivered to the Children's Center
    C. a neglected child requiring shelter, regardless of age, may be delivered to the Bureau of Child Welfare
    D. the Bureau of Child Welfare may determine the shelter to which a foundling may be delivered

4. According to this paragraph, the desk officer shall provide for obtaining shelter for a neglected child, apparently under two years of age, by

   A. directing its delivery to the Children's Center if occurrence is on a Monday between 9 a.m. and 5 p.m.
   B. telephoning the Bureau of Child Welfare if occurrence is on a Sunday
   C. directing its delivery to the Foundling Hospital if occurrence is on a Wednesday at 4 p.m.
   D. telephoning the Bureau of Child Welfare if occurrence is at 10 a.m. on a Friday

4.____

5. According to this paragraph, the desk officer should direct delivery to the Foundling Hospital of any child who is

   A. actually under 2 years of age and requires shelter
   B. apparently under two years of age and is neglected or dependent
   C. actually 2 years of age and is a foundling
   D. apparently under 2 years of age and has been abandoned

5.____

6. A 12-year-old neglected child requiring shelter is brought to a police station on Thursday at 2 p.m. Such a child should be sent to

   A. a shelter selected by the Bureau of Child Welfare
   B. a shelter selected by the desk officer
   C. the Children's Center
   D. the Foundling Hospital when a brother or sister, under 2 years of age, also requires shelter

6.____

Questions 7-9.

DIRECTIONS: Answer Questions 7 to 9 *SOLELY* on the basis of the following statement:

In addition to making the preliminary investigation of crimes, patrolmen should serve as eyes, ears, and legs for the detective division. The patrol division may be used for surveillance, to serve warrants and bring in suspects and witnesses, and to perform a number of routine tasks for the detectives which will increase the time available for tasks that require their special skills and facilities. It is to the advantage of individual detectives, as well as of the detective division, to have patrolmen working in this manner; more cases are cleared by arrest and a greater proportion of stolen property is recovered when, in addition to the detective regularly assigned, a number of patrolmen also work on the case. Detectives may stimulate the interest and participation of patrolmen by keeping them currently informed of the presence, identity, or description, hangouts, associates, vehicles and method of operation of each criminal known to be in the community.

7. According to this paragraph, a patrolman should

   A. assist the detective in certain of his routine functions
   B. be considered for assignment as a detective on the basis of his patrol performance
   C. leave the scene once a detective arrives
   D. perform as much of the detective's duties as time permits

7.____

8. According to this paragraph, patrolmen should aid detectives by 8.___

   A. accepting assignments from detectives which give promise of recovering stolen property
   B. making arrests of witnesses for the detective's interrogation
   C. performing all special investigative work for detectives
   D. producing for questioning individuals who may aid the detective in his investigation

9. According to this paragraph, detectives can keep patrolmen interested by 9.___

   A. ascertaining that patrolmen are doing investigative work properly
   B. having patrolmen directly under his supervision during an investigation
   C. informing patrolmen of the value of their efforts in crime prevention
   D. supplying the patrolmen with information regarding known criminals in the community

Questions 10-11.

DIRECTIONS: Answer Questions 10 and 11 SOLELY on the basis of the following statement:
State motor vehicle registration departments should and do play a vital role in the prevention and detection of automobile thefts. The combatting of theft is, in fact, one of the primary purposes of the registration of motor vehicles. As of recent date, there were approximately 61,309,000 motor vehicles registered in the United States. That same year some 200,000 of them were stolen. All but 6 percent have been or will be recovered. This is a very high recovery ratio compared to the percentage of recovery of other stolen personal property. The reason for this is that automobiles are carefully identified by the manufacturers and carefully registered by many of the states.

10. The CENTRAL thought of this paragraph is that there is a close relationship between the 10.___

    A. number of automobiles registered in the United States and the number stolen
    B. prevention of automobile thefts and the effectiveness of police departments in the United States
    C. recovery of stolen automobiles and automobile registration
    D. recovery of stolen automobiles and of other stolen property

11. According to this paragraph, the high recovery ratio for stolen automobiles is due to 11.___

    A. state registration and manufacturer identification of motor vehicles
    B. successful prevention of automobile thefts by state motor vehicle departments
    C. the fact that only 6% of stolen vehicles are not properly registered
    D. the high number of motor vehicles registered in the United States

Questions 12-15.

DIRECTIONS: Answer Questions 12 to 15 SOLELY on the basis of the following statement:
It is not always understood that the term "physical evidence" embraces any and all objects, living or inanimate. A knife, gun, signature, or burglar tool is immediately recognized as physical evidence. Less often is it considered that dust, microscopic fragments of all types, even an odor, may equally be physical evidence and often the most important of all. It is well established that the most useful types of physical evidence are generally microscopic in dimensions, that is, not noticeable by the eye and, therefore, most likely to be overlooked by

the criminal and by the investigator. For this reason, microscopic evidence persists for months or years after all other evidence has been removed and found inconclusive. Naturally, there are limitations to the time of collecting microscopic evidence as it may be lost or decayed. The exercise of judgment as to the possibility or profit of delayed action in collecting the evidence is a field in which the expert investigator should judge.

12. The *one* of the following which the above paragraph does *NOT* consider to be physical evidence is a

    A. criminal thought
    B. minute speck of dust
    C. raw onion smell
    D. typewritten note

13. According to the above paragraph, the re-checking of the scene of a crime

    A. is *useless* when performed years after the occurrence of the crime
    B. is *advisable* chiefly in crimes involving physical violence
    C. *may turn up* microscopic evidence of value
    D. *should be delayed* if the microscopic evidence is not subject to decay or loss

14. According to the above paragraph, the criminal investigator *should*

    A. give most of his attention to weapons used in the commission of the crime
    B. ignore microscopic evidence until a request is received from the laboratory
    C. immediately search for microscopic evidence and ignore the more visible objects
    D. realize that microscopic evidence can be easily overlooked

15. According to the above paragraph,

    A. a delay in collecting evidence must definitely diminish its value to the investigator
    B. microscopic evidence exists for longer periods of time than other physical evidence
    C. microscopic evidence is generally the most useful type of physical evidence
    D. physical evidence is likely to be overlooked by the criminal and by the investigator

Questions 16-18.

DIRECTIONS: Answer Questions 16 to 18 *SOLELY* on the basis of the following statement:
Sometimes, but not always, firing a gun leaves a residue of nitrate particles on the hands. This fact is utilized in the paraffin test which consists of applying melted paraffin and gauze to the fingers, hands, and wrists of a suspect until a cast of approximately 1/8 of an inch is built up. The heat of the paraffin causes the pores of the skin to open and release any particles embedded in them. The paraffin cast is then removed and tested chemically for nitrate particles. In addition to gunpowder, fertilizers, tobacco ashes, matches, and soot are also common sources of nitrates on the hands.

16. Assume that the paraffin test has been given to a person suspected of firing a gun and that nitrate particles have been found. It would be *CORRECT* to conclude that the suspect

    A. is guilty
    B. is innocent
    C. may be guilty or innocent
    D. is probably guilty

17. In testing for the presence of gunpowder particles on human hands, the characteristic of paraffin which makes it MOST serviceable is that it

   A. causes the nitrate residue left by a fired gun to adhere to the gauze
   B. is waterproof
   C. melts at a low temperature
   D. helps to distinguish between gunpowder nitrates and other types

18. According to the above paragraph, in the paraffin test, the nitrate particles are removed from the pores because the paraffin

   A. enlarges the pores
   B. contracts the pores
   C. reacts chemically with nitrates
   D. dissolves the particles

Questions 19-21.

DIRECTIONS: Answer Questions 19 to 21 SOLELY on the basis of the following statement:
Pickpockets operate most effectively when there are prospective victims in either heavily congested areas or in lonely places. In heavily populated areas, the large number of people about them covers the activities of these thieves. In lonely spots, they have the advantage of working unobserved. The main factor in the pickpocket's success is the selection of the "right" victim, A pickpocket's victim must, at the time of the crime, be inattentive, distracted, or unconscious. If any of these conditions exist, and if the pickpocket is skilled in his operations, the stage is set for a successful larceny. With the coming of winter, the crowds move southward – and so do most of the pickpockets. However, some pickpockets will remain in certain areas all year around. They will concentrate on theater districts, bus and railroad terminals, hotels or large shopping centers. A complete knowledge of the methods of this type of criminal and the ability to recognize them come only from long years of experience in performing patient surveillance and trailing of them. This knowledge is essential for the effective control and apprehension of this type of thief.

19. According to this paragraph, the pickpocket is LEAST likely to operate in a

   A. baseball park with a full capacity attendance
   B. station in an outlying area late at night
   C. moderately crowded dance hall
   D. over-crowded department store

20. According to this paragraph, the one of the following factors which is NOT necessary for the successful operation of the pickpocket is that

   A. he be proficient in the operations required to pick pockets
   B. the "right" potential victims be those who have been the subject of such a theft previously
   C. his operations be hidden from the view of others
   D. the potential victim be unaware of the actions of the pickpocket

21. According to this paragraph, it would be MOST correct to conclude that police officers who are successful in apprehending pickpockets

   A. are generallly those who have had lengthy experience in recognizing all types of criminals
   B. must, by intuition, be able to recognize potential "right" victims

C. must follow the pickpockets in their southward movement
D. must have acquired specific knowledge and skills in this field

Questions 22-23.

DIRECTIONS: Answer Questions 22 and 23 *SOLELY* on the basis of the following statement:
For many years, slums had been recognized as breeding disease, juvenile delinquency, and crime which not only threatened the health and welfare of the people who lived there, but also weakened the structure of society as a whole. As far back as 1834, a sanitary inspection report in the city pointed out the connection between insanitary, overcrowded housing and the spread of epidemics. Down through the years, evidence of slum-produced evils accumulated as the slums themselves continued to spread. This spread of slums was nationwide. Its symptoms and its ill effects were peculiar to no locality, but were characteristic of the country as a whole and imperiled the national welfare.

22. According to this paragraph, people who live in slum dwellings

   A. cause slums to become worse
   B. are threatened by disease and crime
   C. create bad housing
   D. are the chief source of crime in the country

23. According to this paragraph, the effects of juvenile delinquency and crime in slum areas were

   A. to destroy the structure of society
   B. noticeable in all parts of the country
   C. a chief cause of the spread of slums
   D. to spread insanitary conditions in the city

Questions 24-25.

DIRECTIONS: Questions 24 and 25 pertain to the following section of the Penal Law:
Section 1942. A person who, after having been three times convicted within this state, of felonies or attempts to commit felonies, or under the law of any other state, government or country, of crimes which if committed within this state would be felonious, commits a felony, other than murder, first or second degree, or treason, within this state, shall be sentenced upon conviction of such fourth, or subsequent, offense to imprisonment in a state prison for an indeterminate term the minimum of which shall be not less than the maximum term provided for first offenders for the crime for which the individual has been convicted, but, in any event, the minimum term upon conviction for a felony as the fourth, or subsequent, offense, shall be not less than fifteen years, and the maximum thereof shall be his natural life.

24. Under the terms of the above stated portion of Section 1942 of the Penal Law, a person must receive the increased punishment therein provided *if*

   A. he is convicted of a felony and has been three times previously convicted of felonies
   B. he has been three times previously convicted of felonies, regardless of the nature of his present conviction

C. his fourth conviction is for murder, first or second degree, or treason
D. he has previously been convicted three times of murder, first or second degree, or treason

25. Under the terms of the above stated portion of Section 1942 of the Penal Law, a person convicted of a felony for which the penalty is imprisonment for a term not to exceed ten years, and who has been three times previously convicted of felonies in this state, shall be sentenced to a term the *minimum* of which shall be

A. ten years
B. fifteen years
C. indeterminate
D. his natural life

25._____

KEY (CORRECT ANSWERS)

1. B
2. A
3. A
4. D
5. D

6. A
7. A
8. D
9. D
10. C

11. A
12. A
13. C
14. D
15. C

16. C
17. A
18. A
19. C
20. B

21. D
22. B
23. B
24. A
25. B

READING COMPREHENSION
UNDERSTANDING AND INTERPRETING WRITTEN MATERIAL
EXAMINATION SECTION
TEST 1

DIRECTIONS: Each question or incomplete statement is followed by several suggested answers or completions. Select the one that BEST answers the question or completes the statement. *PRINT THE LETTER OF THE CORRECT ANSWER IN THE SPACE AT THE RIGHT.*

Questions 1-3.

DIRECTIONS: Questions 1 through 3 are to be answered SOLELY on the basis of the following passage.

When police officers search for a stolen car, they first check for the color of the car, then for make, model, year, body damage, and finally license number. The first five can be detected from almost any angle, while the recognition of the license number is often not immediately apparent. The serial number and motor number, though less likely to be changed than the easily substituted license number, cannot be observed in initial detection of the stolen car.

1. According to the above passage, the one of the following features which is LEAST readily observed in checking for a stolen car in moving traffic is
    A. license number   B. serial number   C. model
    D. make   E. color

1.____

2. The feature of a car that cannot be determined from most angles of observation is the
    A. make   B. model   C. year
    D. license number E. color

2.____

3. Of the following, the feature of a stolen car that is MOST likely to be altered by a car thief shortly after the car is stolen is the
    A. license number B. motor number   C. color
    D. model   E. minor body damage

3.____

Questions 4-5.

DIRECTIONS: Questions 4 and 5 are to be answered SOLELY on the basis of the following passage.

The racketeer is primarily concerned with business affairs, legitimate or otherwise, and preferably those which are close to the margin of legitimacy. He gets his best opportunities from business organizations which meet the need of large sections of the public for goods or services which are defined as illegitimate by the same public, such as prostitution, gambling, illicit drugs or liquor. In contrast to the thief, the racketeer and the establishments he controls deliver goods and services for money received.

4. From the above passage, it can be deduced that suppression of racketeers is difficult because
   A. victims of racketeers are not guilty of violating the law
   B. racketeers are generally engaged in fully legitimate enterprises
   C. many people want services which are not obtainable through legitimate sources
   D. the racketeers are well organized
   E. laws prohibiting gambling and prostitution are unenforceable

4._____

5. According to the above passage, racketeering, unlike theft, involves
   A. objects of value
   B. payment for goods received
   C. organized gangs
   D. public approval
   E. unlawful activities

5._____

Questions 6-8.

DIRECTIONS: Questions 6 through 8 are to be answered SOLELY on the basis of the following passage.

A number of crimes, such as robbery, assault, rape, certain forms of theft and burglary, are high visibility crimes in that it is apparent to all concerned that they are criminal acts prior to or at the time they are committed. In contrast to these, check forgeries, especially those committed by first offenders, have low visibility. There is little in the criminal act or in the interaction between the check passer and the person cashing the check to identify it as a crime. Closely related to this special quality of the forgery crime is the fact that, while it is formally defined and treated as a felonious or infamous crime, it is formally held by the legally untrained public to be a relatively harmless form of crime.

6. According to the above passage, crimes of *high visibility*
   A. are immediately recognized as crimes by the victim
   B. take place in public view
   C. always involve violence or the threat of violence
   D. usually are committed after dark
   E. can be observed from a distance

6._____

7. According to the above passage,
   A. the public regards check forgery as a minor crime
   B. the law regards check forgery as a minor crime
   C. the law distinguishes between check forgery and other forgery
   D. it is easier to spot inexperienced check forgers than other criminals
   E. it is more difficult to identify check forgers than other criminals

7._____

8. As used in the above passage, an *infamous* crime is
   A. a crime attracting great attention from the public
   B. more serious than a felony
   C. less serious than a felony
   D. more or less than a felony depending upon the surrounding circumstances
   E. the same as a felony

8._____

3 (#1)

Questions 9-11.

DIRECTIONS: Questions 9 through 11 are to be answered SOLELY on the basis of the following passage.

Criminal science is largely the science of identification. Progress in this field has been marked and sometimes very spectacular because new techniques, instruments, and facts flow continuously from the scientists. But the crime laboratories are undermanned, trade secrets still prevail, and inaccurate conclusions are often the results. However, modern gadgets cannot substitute for the skilled intelligent investigator; he must be their master.

9. According to the above passage, criminal science   9.____
   A. excludes the field of investigation
   B. is primarily interested in establishing identity
   C. is based on the equipment used in crime laboratories
   D. uses techniques different from those used in other sciences
   E. is essentially secret in nature

10. Advances in criminal science have been, according to the above passage,   10.____
    A. extremely limited   B. slow but steady
    C. unusually reliable   D. outstanding
    E. infrequently worthwhile

11. A problem that has NOT been overcome completely in crime work is, according   11.____
    to the above passage,
    A. unskilled investigators
    B. the expense of new equipment and techniques
    C. an insufficient number of personnel in crime laboratories
    D. inaccurate equipment used in laboratories
    E. conclusions of the public about the value of this field

Questions 12-14.

DIRECTIONS: Questions 12 through 14 are to be answered SOLELY on the basis of the following passage.

The New York City Police Department will accept for investigation no report of a person missing from his residence, if such residence is located outside of New York City. The person reporting same will be advised to report such fact to the police department of the locality where the missing person lives, which will, if necessary, communicate officially with the New York City Police Department. However, a report will be accepted of a person who is missing from a temporary residence in New York City, but the person making the report will be instructed to make a report also to the police department of the locality where the missing person lives.

12. According to the above passage, a report to the New York City Police Depart-   12.____
    ment of a missing person whose permanent residence is outside of New York
    City will
    A. always be investigated provided that a report is also made to his local
       police authorities

B. never be investigated unless requested officially by his local police authorities
C. be investigated in cases of temporary New York City residence, but a report should always be made to his local police authorities
D. be investigated if the person making the report is a New York City resident
E. always be investigated and a report will be made to the local police authorities by the New York City Police Department

13. Of the following, the MOST likely reason for the procedure described in the above passage is that 13.____
    A. non-residents are not entitled to free police service from New York City
    B. local police authorities would resent interference in their jurisdiction
    C. local police authorities sometimes try to unload their problems on the New York City Police
    D. local police authorities may be better able to conduct an investigation
    E. few persons are erroneously reported as missing

14. Mr. Smith, who lives in Jersey City, and Mr. Jones, who lives in Newark, arrange to meet in New York City, but Mr. Jones doesn't keep the appointment. Mr. Smith telephones Mr. Jones several times the next day and gets no answer. Mr. Smith believes that something has happened to Mr. Jones. According to the above passage, Mr. Smith should apply to the police authorities of 14.____
    A. Jersey City
    B. Newark
    C. Newark and New York City
    D. Jersey City and New York City
    E. Newark, Jersey City, and New York City

Questions 15-17.

DIRECTIONS: Questions 15 through 17 are to be answered SOLELY on the basis of the following passage.

Some early psychologists believed that the basic characteristic of the criminal type was inferiority of intelligence, if not outright feeblemindedness. They were misled by the fact that they had measurements for all kinds of criminals, but, until World War I gave them a draft army sample, they had no information on a comparable group of non-criminal adults. As soon as acceptable measurements could be taken of criminals and a comparable group of non-criminals, concern with feeblemindedness or with low intelligence as a type took on less and less significance in research in criminology.

15. According to the above passage, some early psychologists were in error because they didn't 15.____
    A. distinguish among the various types of criminals
    B. devise a suitable method of measuring intelligence
    C. measure the intelligence of non-criminals as a basis for comparison

D. distinguish between feeblemindedness and inferiority of intelligence
E. clearly define the term *intelligence*

16. The above passage implies that studies of the intelligence of criminals and non-criminals
    A. are useless because it is impossible to obtain comparable groups
    B. are not meaningful because only the less intelligent criminals are detected
    C. indicate that criminals are more intelligent than non-criminals
    D. indicate that criminals are less intelligent than non-criminals
    E. do not indicate that there are any differences between the two groups

17. According to the above passage, studies of the World War I draft gave psychologists vital information concerning
    A. adaptability to army life of criminals and non-criminals
    B. criminal tendencies among draftees
    C. the intelligence scores of large numbers of men
    D. differences between intelligence scores of draftees and volunteers
    E. the behavior of men under abnormal conditions

Questions 18-20.

DIRECTIONS: Questions 18 through 20 are to be answered SOLELY on the basis of the following passage.

The use of a roadblock is simply an adaptation to police practices of the military concept of encirclement. Successful operation of a roadblock plan depends almost entirely on the amount of advance study and planning given to such operations. A thorough and detailed examination of the roads and terrain under the jurisdiction of a given policy agency should be made with the locations of the roadblocks pinpointed in advance. The first principle to be borne in mind in the location of each roadblock is the time element. Its location must be at a point beyond which the fugitive could not have possibly traveled in the time elapsed from the commission of the crime to the arrival of the officers at the roadblock.

18. According to the above passage,
    A. military operations have made extensive use of roadblocks
    B. the military concept of encirclement is an adaptation of police use of roadblocks
    C. the technique of encirclement has been widely used by military forces
    D. a roadblock is generally more effective than encirclement
    E. police use of roadblocks is based on the idea of military encirclement

19. According to the above passage,
    A. the factor of time is the sole consideration in the location of a roadblock
    B. the maximum speed possible in the method of escape is of major importance in roadblock location
    C. the time of arrival of officers at the site of a proposed roadblock is of little importance

6 (#1)

D. if the method of escape is not known, it should be assumed that the escape is by automobile
E. a roadblock should be sited as close to the scene of the crime as the terrain will permit

20. According to the above passage, 20.____
   A. advance study and planning are of minor importance in the success of roadblock operations
   B. a thorough and detailed examination of all roads within a radius of fifty miles should precede the determination of a roadblock location
   C. consideration of terrain features are important in planning the location of roadblocks
   D. the pinpointing of roadblocks should be performed before any advance study is made
   E. a roadblock operation can seldom be successfully undertaken by a single police agency

KEY (CORRECT ANSWERS)

1.	B	11.	C
2.	D	12.	C
3.	A	13.	D
4.	C	14.	B
5.	B	15.	C
6.	A	16.	E
7.	A	17.	C
8.	E	18.	E
9.	B	19.	B
10.	D	20.	C

TEST 2

DIRECTIONS: Each question or incomplete statement is followed by several suggested answers or completions. Select the one that BEST answers the question or completes the statement. *PRINT THE LETTER OF THE CORRECT ANSWER IN THE SPACE AT THE RIGHT.*

Questions 1-3.

DIRECTIONS: Questions 1 through 3 are to be answered SOLELY on the basis of the following passage.

Modern police science may be said to have three phases. The first phase embraces the identification of living and dead persons. The second embraces the field work carried out by specially trained detectives at the scene of the crime. The third embraces methods used in the police laboratory to examine and analyze clues and traces discovered in the course of the investigation. While modern police science has had a striking influence on detective work and will surely further enhance its effectiveness, the time-honored methods and practical detective work will always be important. The time-honored methods, that is knowledge of methods used by criminals, patience, tact, industry, thoroughness, and imagination, will always be requisites for successful detective work.

1. According to the above passage, we may expect modern police science to 1._____
    A. help detective work more and more
    B. become more and more scientific
    C. depend less and less on the time-honored methods
    D. bring together the many different approaches to detective work
    E. play a less important role in detective work

2. According to the above passage, a knowledge of the procedures used by criminals is 2._____
    A. solely an element of the modern police science approach to detective work
    B. related to the identification of persons
    C. not related to detective field work
    D. related to methods used in the police laboratory
    E. an element of the traditional approach to detective work

3. Modern police science and practical detective work, according to the above passage, 3._____
    A. when used together can only lead to confusion
    B. are based distinctly different theories of detective work
    C. have had strikingly different influence on detective work
    D. should both be used for successful detective work
    E. lead usually to similar results

Questions 4-7.

DIRECTIONS: Questions 4 through 7 are to be answered SOLELY on the basis of the following passage.

A member of the force shall render reasonable aid to a sick or injured person. He shall summon an ambulance, if necessary, by telephoning the communications bureau of the borough, who shall notify the precinct concerned. If possible, he shall wait in full view of the arriving ambulance and take necessary action to direct the responding doctor or attendant to the patient, without delay. If the ambulance does not arrive in twenty minutes, he shall send in a second call. However, if the sick person is in his or her own home, a member of the force, before summoning an ambulance, will ascertain whether such person is willing to be taken to a hospital for treatment.

4. According to the above passage, if a patrolman wants to get an ambulance for a sick person, he should telephone
    A. the precinct concerned
    B. only if the sick person is in his home
    C. the nearest hospital
    D. only if the sick person is not in his home
    E. the borough communications bureau

5. According to the above passage, if a patrolman telephones for an ambulance and none arrives within twenty minutes, he should
    A. ask the injured person if he is willing to be taken to a hospital
    B. call the borough communications bureau
    C. call the precinct concerned
    D. attempt to give the injured person such assistance as he may need
    E. call the nearest hospital

6. A patrolman is called to help a woman who has fallen in her own home and has apparently broken her leg.
    According to the above passage, he should
    A. ask her if she wants to go to a hospital
    B. try to set her leg if it is necessary
    C. call for an ambulance at once
    D. attempt to get a doctor as quickly as possible
    E. not attempt to help the woman in any way before competent medical aid arrives

7. A man falls from a window into the backyard of an apartment house. Assume that you are a patrolman and that you are called to assist this man.
    According to the above passage, after you have called for an ambulance and comforted the injured man as much as you can, you should
    A. wait in front of the house for the ambulance
    B. ask the injured man if he wishes to go to the hospital for treatment
    C. remain with the injured man until the ambulance arrives
    D. send a bystander to direct the nearest doctor to the patient
    E. not ask the man to explain how the accident happened

Questions 8-10.

DIRECTIONS: Questions 8 through 10 are to be answered SOLELY on the basis of the following passage.

What is required is a program that will protect our citizens and their property from criminal and antisocial acts, will effectively restrain and reform juvenile delinquents, and will prevent the further development of antisocial behavior. Discipline and punishment of offenders must necessarily play an important part in any such program. Serious offenders cannot be mollycoddled merely because they are under twenty-one. Restraint and punishment necessarily follow serious antisocial acts. But punishment, if it is to be effective, must be a planned part of a more comprehensive program of treating delinquency.

8. The one of the following goals NOT included among those listed above is to 8._____
    A. stop young people from defacing public property
    B. keep homes from being broken into
    C. develop an intra-city boys' baseball league
    D. change juvenile delinquents into useful citizens
    E. prevent young people from developing antisocial behavior patterns

9. According to the above passage, punishment is 9._____
    A. not satisfactory in any program dealing with juvenile delinquents
    B. the most effective means by which young vandals and hooligans can be reformed
    C. not used sufficiently when dealing with serious offenders who are under twenty-one
    D. of value in reducing juvenile delinquency only if it is part of a complete program
    E. most effective when it does not relate to specific antisocial acts

10. With respect to serious offenders who are under twenty-one, the above passage suggests that they 10._____
    A. be mollycoddled
    B. be dealt with as part of a comprehensive program to punish mature criminals
    C. should be punished
    D. be prevented, by brute force if necessary, from performing antisocial acts
    E. be treated as delinquent children who require more love than punishment

Questions 11-14.

DIRECTIONS: Questions 11 through 14 are to be answered SOLELY on the basis of the following passage.

In all cases of homicide, members of the Police Department who investigate will make every effort to obtain statements from dying persons. Such statements are of the greatest importance to the District Attorney. In many cases, there may be a failure to solve the crime if they are not taken. The principle element to be considered in taking the declaration of a dying person is his mental attitude. In order to be admissible in evidence, the person must have no hope of recovery. The patient will be fully interrogated on that point before a statement is taken.

11. In cases of homicide, according to the above passage, members of the police force will
    A. try to change the mental attitude of the dying person
    B. attempt to obtain a statement from the dying person
    C. not give the information they obtain directly to the District Attorney
    D. be careful not to injure the dying person unnecessarily
    E. prevent unauthorized persons from taking dying declarations

11.____

12. The mental attitude of the person making the dying statement is of great importance because it can determine, according to the above passage, whether the
    A. victim should be interrogated in the presence of witnesses
    B. victim will be willing to make a statement of any kind
    C. victim has been forced to make the statement
    D. statement will tell the District Attorney who committed the crime
    E. statement can be used as evidence

12.____

13. District Attorneys find that statements of a dying person are important, according to the above passage, because
    A. it may be that the victim will recover and refuse to testify
    B. they are important elements in determining the mental attitude of the victim
    C. they present a point of view
    D. it may be impossible to punish the criminal without such a statement
    E. dead men tell no tales

13.____

14. A well-known gangster is found dying from a bullet wound. The patrolman first on the scene, in the presence of witnesses, tells the man that he is going to die and asks, *Who shot you?* The gangster says, *Jones shot me, but he hasn't killed me. I'll live to get him.* He then falls back dead.
    According to the above passage, this statement is
    A. *admissible* in evidence; the man was obviously speaking the truth
    B. *not admissible* in evidence; the man obviously did not believe that he was dying
    C. *admissible* in evidence; there were witnesses to the statement
    D. *not admissible* in evidence; the victim did not sign any statement and the evidence is merely hearsay
    E. *admissible* in evidence; there was no time to interrogate the victim

14.____

Questions 15-17.

DIRECTIONS: Questions 15 through 17 are to be answered SOLELY on the basis of the following passage.

The factors contributing to crime and delinquency are varied and complex. The home and its immediate environment have been found to be crucial in determining the behavior patterns of the individual, and criminality can frequently be traced to faulty family relationships and a bad neighborhood. But in the search for a clearer understanding of the underlying causes of delinquent and criminal behavior, the total environment must be taken into consideration.

15. According to the above passage, family relationships   15._____
    A. tend to become faulty in bad neighborhoods
    B. are important in determining the actions of honest people as well as criminals
    C. are the only important element in the understanding of causes of delinquency
    D. are determined by the total environment
    E. of criminals are understandable only in terms of the behavior patterns of the individuals concerned

16. According to the above passage, the causes of crime and delinquency are   16._____
    A. not simple   B. not meaningless
    C. meaningless   D. simple
    E. always understandable

17. According to the above passage, faulty family relationships frequently are   17._____
    A. responsible for varied and complex results
    B. caused by differences
    C. caused when one or both parents have a criminal behavior pattern
    D. independent of the total environment
    E. the cause of criminal acts

Questions 18-20.

DIRECTIONS: Questions 18 through 20 are to be answered SOLELY on the basis of the following passage.

A change in the specific problems which confront the police and in the methods for dealing with them has taken place in the last few decades. The automobile is a two-way symbol of this change in policing. It menaces every city with a complicated traffic problem and has speeded up the process of committing a crime and making a getaway, but at the same time has increased the effectiveness of police operations. However, the major concern of police departments continues to be the antisocial or criminal actions and behavior of human beings.

18. On the basis of the above passage, it can be stated that for the most part in   18._____
    the past few decades, the specific problems of a police force
    A. have changed but the general problems have not
    B. as well as the general problems have changed
    C. have remained the same but the general problems have changed
    D. as well as the general problems have remained the same
    E. have caused changes in the general problems

19. According to the above passage, advances in science and industry have, in general, made the police
    A. operations less effective from the overall point of view
    B. operations more effective from the overall point of view
    C. abandon older methods of solving police problems
    D. concern themselves more with the antisocial acts of human beings
    E. concern themselves less with the antisocial acts of human beings

20. The automobile is a *two-way symbol*, according to the above passage, because its use
    A. has speeded up getting to, and away from, the scene of a crime
    B. both helps and hurts police operations
    C. introduces a new antisocial act—traffic violation—and does away with criminals like horse thieves
    D. both increases and decreases speed by introducing traffic problems
    E. helps people get to the city but prevents them from moving once they are there

KEY (CORRECT ANSWERS)

1.	A	11.	B
2.	E	12.	E
3.	D	13.	D
4.	E	14.	B
5.	B	15.	B
6.	A	16.	A
7.	A	17.	E
8.	C	18.	A
9.	D	19.	B
10.	C	20.	B

ARITHMETICAL REASONING

EXAMINATION SECTION
TEST 1

DIRECTIONS: Each question or incomplete statement is followed by several suggested answers or completions. Select the one that BEST answers the question or completes the statement. *PRINT THE LETTER OF THE CORRECT ANSWER IN THE SPACE AT THE RIGHT.*

1. Assume that a certain state set aside 40% of the state gasoline tax for use by its cities in solving traffic problems. This year, there were 800,000,000 gallons of gasoline used in that state, and the tax was 12 cents per gallon.
   The amount which the cities received as their share this year was

   A. $3,840,000 B. $9,600,000
   C. $38,400,000 D. $96,000,000

   1.___

2. Suppose that a radio motor patrol car costs the municipality $11,075 less a discount of 15%. After five years, it is sold at public auction for $1,750.
   The annual cost of the car to the municipality, excluding other costs, was *most nearly*

   A. $1,500 B. $1,750 C. $2,000 D. $2,250

   2.___

3. A police car on a special assignment made a round trip to another city 186 miles away. For the entire trip, it used 24.8 gallons of gasoline, costing $3.70 a gallon.
   The cost for gasoline per mile was *most nearly*

   A. $.09 B. $.18 C. $.24 D. $.31

   3.___

4. The city has been testing various types of gasoline for economy and efficiency. It has been found that a police radio patrol car can travel 18 miles on a gallon of gasoline Brand A costing $4.50 a gallon and 15 miles on a gallon of gasoline Brand B costing $3.96 a gallon.
   For a trip of 900 miles, Brand B will cost _____ Brand A.

   A. $12.60 more than B. $12.60 less than
   C. $126.00 more than D. the same as

   4.___

5. A Police Department helicopter has been flying for 3 hours at an average speed of 40 miles per hour in search of an overturned boat. The helicopter started out with 210 gallons of fuel, used an average of 60 gallons of fuel per hour, and is now twenty miles from the airport.
   The MAXIMUM amount of time that the pilot can spare in his search before returning to the airport is

   A. 1 hour B. 1 1/2 hours C. 2 hours D. no more time

   5.___

6. There were 25% more arrests for shoplifting in a congested business area in 2004 than in 2006, and 10% less in 2006 than in 2002.
   If the number of such arrests in 2002 was 150, then the number of such arrests in 2004 was *most nearly*

   A. 160 B. 170 C. 180 D. 205

   6.___

147

7. The cost of operating 20 radio patrol cars assigned to a certain district was carefully checked during the past year. The cost of running 4 of the cars was $525 each, the cost of running 5 of the cars was $750 each, the cost or running 7 of the cars was $975 each, and the remainder cost $1,125 each to run.
The AVERAGE operating cost per car was *most nearly*

   A. $820   B. $840   C. $860   D. $880

8. A suspect arrested in New Jersey is being turned over by New Jersey authorities to two Nassau County police officers for a crime committed in Nassau County. The Nassau County, N.Y. officers receive their prisoner at a point 18 1/2 miles from their precinct station house, and travel directly toward their destination at an average speed of 40 miles an hour, except for a delay of 10 minutes at one point because of a traffic tie-up. The time it should take the officers to reach their destination is *most nearly* _____ minutes.

   A. 18   B. 22   C. 32   D. 38

9. A parking lot is to be set up near a new baseball stadium with provision for 3,750 cars. Each car requires 160 square feet of parking space; also, additional space equal to 30% of car space requirements is needed for driveways. Four sites for the lot are being considered. Site A is 1,000 feet long and 800 feet wide. Site B is 900 feet long and 875 feet wide. Site C is 800 feet long and 925 feet wide. Site D is 950 feet long and 850 feet wide. On the basis of the above information, the SMALLEST site which will provide sufficient space is Site

   A. A   B. B   C. C   D. D

10. As a result of a series of robberies of small jewelry establishments, an intensified check of 364 pawn shops has been ordered. Four detectives have been assigned to this detail. At the end of 3 days of 7 hours each, they have checked 168 pawn shops. In order to speed up the investigation, three more detectives are assigned at this point.
If they worked at the same rate, the number of ADDITIONAL 7-hour days it would take to complete the job is *most nearly* _____ days.

   A. 2   B. 4   C. 6   D. 8

KEY (CORRECT ANSWERS)

1. C
2. A
3. C
4. A
5. D

6. B
7. C
8. D
9. B
10. A

SOLUTIONS TO PROBLEMS

1. ANSWER: C.
   800,000,000 x .12 = $96,000,000
   $96,000,000 x .40 = $38,400,000

2. ANSWER: A. $1,500

   $11,075
   × .15
   ─────
   55375
   11075
   ─────
   $1661.25 (discount)

   $11075 - $1661.25 = $9413.75 (original cost of car)
   $9413.75 - $1750 = $7663.75 (cost of car after 5 years)
   $7663.75 ÷ 5 = $1532.75 (annual cost of car)

3. ANSWER: C. $.24
   24.8 x $3.70 = $91.76 (total cost of gasoline)
   186 x 2 = 372 miles (total distance round trip)
   ∴ $91.76 ÷ 372 = $.24 (cost for gasoline per mile)

4. ANSWER: A. $12.60 more than Brand A
   Brand A: 900 ÷ 18 x 4.50 = $225.00
   Brand B: 900 ÷ 15 x 3.96 = $237.60
   ∴ Brand B will cost $12.60 more than Brand A

5. ANSWER: D. no more time
   Helicopter has already used up 180 gallons of the 210 gallons
   (3 hours at 60 gallons of fuel per hour)
   Since its average speed is 40 m.p.h., it will take one-half hour
   to complete the 20 miles to the airport.
   In 1/2 hour, it will use up another 30 gallons of fuel or the
   remainder of the 210 gallons.
   Therefore, the pilot can spare no more time.

6. ANSWER: B. 170
   2002: 150
   2006: 150 - 15 (10% of 150) = 135
   2004: 135 + 1/4 x 135 (25% more than in 2006)
   135 + 33 3/4 = 168 3/4

7. ANSWER: C. $860

4 at $525 =	$2100
5 at $750 =	3750
7 at $975 =	6825
4 (20 -16 = 4, remainder) at $1125 =	4500
	$17,175 (total operating cost)

$17,175 (total operating cost)
$17,175 ÷ 20 = average operating cost per car
　　　　= $858.75

8. ANSWER: D. 38 minutes

Average speed of 40 miles an hour = 2/3 mile per minute
　　　　　　　　　　　　　　　　(40 mph 60 min.)

Distance ÷ Rate　　　　　　　　= Time
18 1/2 (miles) ÷ 2/3 (mile per minute = 37/2 ÷ 2/3
　　　　　　　　　　　　　　= 37/2 x 3/2 = 111/4 = 27 3/4 minutes
27 3/4 + 10 (delay) = 37 3/4 minutes

9. ANSWER: B. Site B

3750 x 160 =　　600,000 sq. ft. (parking space)
600,000 x .30 =　180,000 sq. ft. (driveways)
　　　　　　　　780,000 sq. ft. (total needed for parking lot)

Site A:	1000	x	800	=	800,000	sq. ft.
Site B:	900	x	875	=	787,500	sq. ft.
Site C:	800	x	925	=	740,000	sq. ft.
Site D:	950	x	850	=	807,500	sq. ft.

10. ANSWER: A. 2 days

$168 ÷ 3 (days) = 56 checked per day (by 4 detectives)
4 detectives do 1 day's work = 56
3 detectives added do 1 3/4 day's work = 56 x 7/4 = 98 (in one day by all seven working together)
364 - 168 = 196 (remain to be checked)
∴ 196 ÷ 98 = 2 days

TEST 2

DIRECTIONS: Each question or incomplete statement is followed by several suggested answers or completions. Select the one that BEST answers the question or completes the statement. *PRINT THE LETTER OF THE CORRECT ANSWER IN THE SPACE AT THE RIGHT.*

1. During the first nine months of this year, an officer spent an average of $270 a month. In October and November, he spent an average of $315 a month. In December, he spent $385.
   His average monthly spending during the year was *most nearly*

   A. $254   B. $287   C. $323   D. $3,000

2. In 2005, there were 8,270 arrests in a certain city. In 2006, the number of arrests increased by 12 1/2%. In 2007, the number of arrests decreased 5% from the 2006 figures. The number of arrests in 2007 was *most nearly*

   A. 8,840   B. 9,770   C. 6,870   D. 7,600

3. Assume that parking space is to be provided for 25% of the tenants in a new housing development. The project will have five 6-story buildings, having seven tenants on each floor, and eight 11-story buildings, having eight tenants on each floor.
   The number of parking spaces needed is *most nearly*

   A. 215   B. 230   C. 700   D. 895

4. A stolen vehicle traveling at 60 miles per hour passes by a police car which is standing still with the engine running. The police car immediately starts out in pursuit, and one minute later, having covered a distance of half a mile, it reaches a speed of 90 miles per hour and continues at this speed.
   After the stolen vehicle passes the police car, the police car will overtake it in _____ minute(s).

   A. 1   B. 1 1/2   C. 2   D. 3

5. A police officer found his 42-hour work week was divided as follows: 1/6 of his time in investigating incidents on his patrol post; 1/2 of his time patrolling his post; and 1/8 of his time in special traffic duty. The rest of his time was devoted to assignments at precinct headquarters. The percentage of his work week which was spent at precinct headquarters is *most nearly*

   A. 10%   B. 15%   C. 20%   D. 25%

6. In 2006, the Department of Sanitation towed away 8,430 cars which were abandoned or illegally parked on city streets. If the value of the abandoned cars was $1,038,200 and that of the illegally parked cars was $6,234,800, then the AVERAGE value of one of the towed-away cars was *most nearly*

   A. $400   B. $720   C. $860   D. $1,100

7. Two percent of all school children are problem children. Some 80% of these problem children become delinquents, and about 80% of the delinquent children become criminals. If the school population is 1,000,000 children, the number of this group who will eventually become criminals, according to this analysis, is

   A. 12,800   B. 1,280   C. 640   D. 128

2 (#2)

8. A patrol car began a trip with 12 gallons of gasoline in the tank and ended with 74 gallons. The car travelled 17.3 miles for each gallon of gasoline. During the trip, gasoline was bought for $20.88 at $2.61 per gallon.
The TOTAL NUMBER of miles travelled during this trip was, *most nearly*

   A. 79 B. 196 C. 216 D. 229

9. A radio motor patrol car finds it necessary to travel at 90 miles per hour for a period of 1 minute and 40 seconds. The NUMBER of miles which the car travels during this period is

   A. 1 5/6 B. 2 C. 2 1/2 D. 3 3/4

10. A radio motor patrol car has to travel a distance of 15 miles in an emergency. If it does the first two-thirds of the distance at 40 m.p.h. and the last third at 60 m.p.h., the TOTAL NUMBER of minutes required for the entire run is *most nearly*

    A. 15 B. 20 C. 22 1/2 D. 25

KEY (CORRECT AMSWERS)

1. B
2. A
3. B
4. C
5. C

6. C
7. A
8. C
9. C
10. B

SOLUTIONS TO PROBLEMS

1. ANSWER: B. $287

    First 9 months at $270 = $ 2430
    October   at 315 =   315
    November   at 315 =   315
    December   at 385 =   385
    $ 3445 (total for year)

    ∴ $3445 ÷ 12 = $287.08 (average monthly spending during the year)

2. ANSWER: A. 8840

    Given   2005   8270
            2006   + 12 1/2% of 2005
            2007   - 5% of 2006
    Solving 12 1/2% = 1/8; 1/8 x 8270   = 1035
             2005 = 1035 + 8270   = 9305
             .05 x 9305 = 465.25
             2006 = 9305 - 465.25   = 8839.75

3. ANSWER: B. 230

    5 six-story buildings at 7 tenants each floor = 5x6x7 = 210
    8 eleven-story buildings at 8 tenants each floor = 8 x 11 x 8 = 704
    210 + 704 = 914 (total number of tenants)
    ∴ 1/2 (25%) x 914 = 228.5 (number of parking spaces needed)

4. ANSWER: C. 2 minutes

    Given   Stolen car: travels 60 miles per hour; will have
                             travelled 1 mile in 1 minute (60(miles) ÷
                             60 (minutes)
               Police car: travels 1/2 mile in first minute; thereafter,
                             travels at rate of 1 1/2 miles per minute
                             (90 miles per hour (rate) ÷ 60 (minutes)
    Solution   Stolen car: in 3 minutes will have travelled 3 miles
                             (3x1 mph)
               Police car: in first minute covers distance of 1/2 mile;
                             in next two minutes will have covered an
                             additional 3 miles (2 x 1 1/2 miles)

5. ANSWER: C. 20%

    42 x 1/6 = 7 hrs.
    42 x 1/2 = 21 hrs.
    42 x 1/8 = $5\frac{1}{4}$ hrs.
    _____
              $33\frac{1}{4}$ hrs.

    42 - 33 1/4 = 8 3/4 hrs. (time spent at precinct headquarters)

    ∴ 8 3/4 ÷ 42 = 35/4 ÷ 42 = 35/4 x 1/42 = 35/168 = .20$^+$

6. ANSWER: C. $860
   $1,038,200 + $6,234,800 = $7,273,000
   $7,273,000 ÷ 8430 = 862^+$

7. ANSWER: A. 12,800
   $1,000,000   x   .02   =   20,000   (number of problem children)
       20,000   x   .80   =   16,000   (number of delinquent children)
       16,000   x   .80   =   12,800   (number of criminals)

8. ANSWER: C. 216
   Patrol car began trip with 12 gallons
   Added to tank, while on trip, 8 gallons ($20.88 ÷ $2.61(per gallon) Therefore, the patrol car had a total of 20 gallons for the trip. If 7 1/2 gallons remained at end of trip, therefore
   ∴ 12 1/2 gallons had been used up on the trip.
   12 1/2 (gallons) x 17.3 (miles for each gallon) = total number of miles travelled = 216.25

9. ANSWER: C. 2 1/2
   Rate of 90 = 1 1/2 miles per minute (90 (miles) 4 ÷ 60 (minutes)
   1 minute and 40 seconds = 1 2/3 minutes
   ∴ 1 1/2 x 1 2/3 = 3/2 x 5/3 = 15/6 = 2 1/2

10. ANSWER: B. 20
    40 m.p.h. = 2/3 mile per minute (40 (miles) 60 (minutes)
    ∴ 2/3 x 15 ÷ 2/3 = 10 ÷ 2/3 = 10 x 3/2 = 15 minutes
    60 m.p.h. = 1 mile per minute (60 (miles) ÷ 60 (minutes)
    ∴ 1/3 x 15 1 = 5 minutes
    15 minutes + 5 minutes = 20 minutes

TEST 3

DIRECTIONS: Each question or incomplete statement is followed by several suggested answers or completions. Select the one that BEST answers the question or completes the statement. *PRINT THE LETTER OF THE CORRECT ANSWER IN THE SPACE AT THE RIGHT.*

1. A patrol car had 11 1/2 gallons of gasoline at the beginning of a trip of 196 miles and 5 1/2 gallons at the end of the trip. During the trip, gasoline was bought for $19.53 at a cost of $3.90 per gallon.
   The AVERAGE number of miles driven per gallon of gasoline is *most nearly*

   A. 14   B. 14.5   C. 18   D. 25.5

2. There are 15 police cadets assigned to a certain operation. One-third earn $21,000 per year, three earn $22,050 per year, one earns $24,675 per year, and the rest earn $27,905 per year.
   The AVERAGE annual salary of these policemen is *most nearly*

   A. $23,750   B. $24,000   C. $24,250   D. $24,500

3. In 2006, the cost of patrol car maintenance and repair was $2,500 more than in 2005, representing an increase of 10%.
   The cost of patrol car maintenance and repair in 2006 was *most nearly*

   A. $2,750   B. $22,500   C. $25,000   D. $27,500

4. A police precinct has an assigned strength of 180 men. Of this number, 25% are not available for duty due to illness, vacations, and other reasons. Of those who are available for duty, 1/3 are assigned outside of the precinct for special emergency duty.
   The ACTUAL available strength of the precinct in terms of men immediately available for precinct duty is

   A. 45   B. 60   C. 90   D. 135

5. Five police officers are taking target practice. The number of rounds fired by each and the percentage of perfect shots is as follows:
   Officer R   80   rounds fired;   30%   perfect shots
           S   70   rounds fired;   40%   perfect shots
           T   75   rounds fired;   60%   perfect shots
           U   92   rounds fired;   25%   perfect shots
           V   96   rounds fired;   66 2/3%   perfect shots
   The AVERAGE number of perfect shots fired by them is *most nearly*

   A. 30   B. 36   C. 42   D. 80

6. A dozen five-gallon cans of paint weigh 492 pounds. Each can, when empty, weighs 3 pounds.
   The weight of one gallon of paint is *most nearly* _____ lbs.

   A. 5   B. 6 1/2   C. 7 1/2   D. 8

7. A parade is marching up an average of 60 city blocks. A sample count of the number of people watching the parade on one side of the street in the block is taken, first, in a block near the end of the parade, and then in a block at the middle; the former count is 4000, the latter is 6000. If the average for the entire parade is assumed to be the average of the two samples, then the ESTIMATED number of persons watching the entire parade is *most nearly*

    A. 240,000   B. 300,000   C. 480,000   D. 600,000

8. Suppose that the revenue from parking meters in the city was 5% greater in 2005 than in 2004, and 2% less in 2006 than in 2005.
    If the revenue in 2004 was $1,500,000, then the revenue in 2006 was

    A. $1,541,500   B. $1,542,000
    C. $1,542,500   D. $1,543,000

9. A radio motor patrol car completes a ten-mile trip in twenty minutes.
    If it does one-half the distance at a speed of twenty miles an hour, its speed, in miles per hour, for the remainder of the distance must be

    A. 30   B. 40   C. 50   D. 60

10. A public beach has two parking areas. Their capacities are in the ratio of two to one and, on a certain day, are filled to 60% and 40% of capacity, respectively. The entire parking facilities of the beach on that day are *most nearly* _____ filled.

    A. 38%   B. 43%   C. 48%   D. 53%

KEY (CORRECT ANSWERS)

1. C
2. C
3. D
4. C
5. B

6. C
7. D
8. D
9. D
10. D

SOLUTIONS TO PROBLEMS

1. ANSWER: C. 18
   Gasoline: At beginning of trip -11 1/2 gallons
   Bought gasoline for $19.53 at $3.90 per gallon; or
   $$19.53 \div 3.90 = 5 \text{ gal.}$$
   11 1/2 + 5 = 16 1/2 gallons (total)
   16 1/2 - 5 1/2 = 11 (number of gallons used up on the trip)
   ∴ 196 ÷ 11 = 17.8 = 18 (average number of miles
   driven per gallon.

2. ANSWER: C. $24,250
5 (1/3 x 15)	at $21,000	=	$105,000
3	at 22,050	=	66,150
1	at 24,675	=	24,675
6 (rest)	at 27,905	=	167,430

   ∴ $363,255 ÷ 15 = $24,250+ (average annual salary)

3. ANSWER: D. $27,500
   In 2006, the cost of $2,500 = an increase of 10% over 2005.
   Therefore, the cost of maintenance and repair in 2005 = $25,000 ($2,500 is 10% of $25,000).
   Hence, the cost in 2006 was $25,000 + $2,500 = $27,500.

4. ANSWER: C. 90
   Not available for duty: 1/4 (25%) x 180 = 45
   Available for duty: 1/3 x 135 (180 - 45) = 45
   ∴ 45 + 45 = 90 (actual available strength of the precinct)

5. ANSWER: B. 36
R	=	.30 x 80	=	24
S	=	.40 x 70	=	28
T	=	.60 x 75	=	45
U	=	.25 x 92	=	23
V	=	2/3(.66 2/3) x 96	=	64

   184 (total perfect shots)
   ∴ 184 ÷ 5 = 35 4/5 (average number of perfect shots)

6. ANSWER: C. 7 1/2 lbs.
   12 x 3 = 36 pounds (weight of a dozen 5-gallon cans when empty)
   Hence, 492 - 36 = 456 lbs. (weight of the paint only in the
   dozen 5-gallon cans)
   ∴ 456 ÷ 60 (number of gallons in a dozen 5-gallon cans)
   = 7.6 lbs. (weight of one gallon of paint)

7. ANSWER: D. 600,000
   4000 + 6000 = 10,000 (total for one side of the street)
   10,000 ÷ 2 = 5,000 (average for one side of the street)
   5,000 x 2 = 10,000 (average for both sides of the street)
   ∴ 60 (blocks) x 10,000 (people) = 600,000

4 (#3)

8. ANSWER: D. $1,543,500
   2004: $1,500,000
   2005: $1,500,000 + .05 x $1,500,000   = $1,500,000 + $75,000 =
                                              $1,575,000
   2006: $1,575,000 - .02 x $1,575,000   = $1,575,000 - $31,500 =
                                              $1,543,500

9. ANSWER: D. 60
   10 miles are completed in a total of 20 minutes. 5 miles (1/2 of 10 miles) at 20 miles an hour = 1 mile in 3 minutes or
   5 miles in 15 minutes
   ∴ the remaining 5 miles must be completed in 5 minutes, or a rate of one mile a minute, which is equal to a speed of 60 miles per hour

10. ANSWER: D. 53% filled
    If the capacities of the parking areas are in the ratio of 2:1, then one has 2/3 of the total capacity, and the other has 1/3.

    Then, 2/3 x .60 = .40
          1/3 x .40 = .13 1/3
                      .53 1/3

ARITHMETICAL REASONING

EXAMINATION SECTION
TEST 1

DIRECTIONS: Each question or incomplete statement is followed by several suggested answers or completions. Select the one that BEST answers the question or completes the statement. *PRINT THE LETTER OF THE CORRECT ANSWER IN THE SPACE AT THE RIGHT.*

1. Two patrol cars hurry to the scene of an accident from different directions. The first proceeds at the rate of 45 miles per hour and arrives in four minutes. Although the second car travels over a route which is three-fourths of a mile longer, it arrives at the scene only a half minute later.
   The speed of the second car, expressed in miles per hour, is

   A. 50 B. 55 C. 60 D. 65

   1.____

2. A motorcycle policeman issued 72 traffic summonses in January, 60 in February, and 83 in March.
   In order to average 75 summonses per month for the four months of January, February, March, and April, during
   April he will have to issue _____ summonses.

   A. 80 B. 85 C. 90 D. 95

   2.____

3. In a unit of the Police Department to which 40 patrolmen are assigned, the sick report during the year was as follows:
   1 was absent 8 days   5 were absent 3 days each
   4 were absent 5 days each   10 were absent 2 days each
   8 were absent 4 days each   5 were absent 1 day each
   The average number of days on sick report for all the members of this unit is MOST NEARLY

   A. 1/2 B. 1 C. 2 1/2 D. 3

   3.____

4. For a certain police department, the average officer is entitled to two days off per week, gets 18 vacation days per year, takes 11 days for sick leave per year, and spends approximately 4 days per year (on the average) on training assignments. A certain shift commander has 20 men assigned to his shift for field patrol.
   Which one of the following is MOST NEARLY the average number of man-days per week that the shift commander has available to him for assignment?
   _____ man-days.

   A. 62.5 B. 75.0 C. 84.0 D. 87.5

   4.____

5. A car speeds through the toll entrance of a 2 1/4 mile long bridge without paying the toll and reaches the other end of the bridge 1 minute and 30 seconds later.
   The car was traveling MOST NEARLY at a rate of _____ miles per hour.

   A. 60 B. 70 C. 80 D. 90

   5.____

6. During one week, 21,500 vehicles passed through the toll booths of a certain bridge. Of these, 550 were buses, 2,230 were trucks, and the rest were passenger cars. The toll charges were $1.00 for a passenger car, $2.00 for a truck, and $4.00 for a bus.
The TOTAL income for the week was

   A. $23,100   B. $25,380   C. $29,300   D. $31,300

7. A bullet fired from a revolver travels 100 feet the first second, and each succeeding second it travels a distance 10% less than during the immediately preceding second. The number of feet the bullet will have traveled at the end of the fourth second is MOST NEARLY

   A. 272   B. 320   C. 344   D. 360

8. An officer receives a uniform allowance of $250 a year in a lump sum. Of this amount, he spends $90 for a winter jacket and 40% of the remainder for two pairs of trousers. The officer now wishes to buy a winter overcoat which costs $120.
The percentage of the purchase price of the overcoat by which he will be short is

   A. 20%   B. 25%   C. 48%   D. 60%

9. It has been suggested that small light cars be used for certain kinds of police work. These light vehicles can run 30 miles per gallon of gasoline as contrasted with standard cars which run only 15 miles per gallon. Assume gasoline costs the city $3.75 per gallon During 9,000 miles of travel, use of the small light car in preference to the standard car would result in a saving in gasoline costs of MOST NEARLY

   A. $1,125   B. $15,000   C. $1,875   D. $2,250

10. Out of a total of 34,750 felony complaints in 2007, 14,200 involved burglary. In 2006, there was a total of 32,300 felony complaints of which 12,800 were burglary.
Of the increase in felonies from 2006 to 2007, the increase in burglaries comprised APPROXIMATELY

    A. 27%   B. 37%   C. 47%   D. 57%

11. A certain city department has two offices which issue permits, one office handling twice as many applicants as the other. The smaller office grants permits to 40% of its applicants. The larger office handling twice as many applicants grants permits to 60% of its applicants. If there were 900 applicants at both offices together on a given day, the total number of permits granted by both offices would be MOST NEARLY

    A. 420   B. 450   C. 480   D. 510

12. You are making a report on the number of incoming calls handled by two different switchboards. Over a five-day period, the total count of incoming calls per day for both switchboards together was 2,773. The average number of incoming calls per day for Switchboard A was 301.
You cannot find one day's tally for Switchboard B, but the total for the other four days for Switchboard B comes to 1,032.
Determine from this how many incoming calls must have been reported on the missing tally for Switchboard B?

    A. 236   B. 258   C. 408   D. 1,440

13. Assume that one-page notices for distribution may be reproduced by photocopy or by stencil. The cost for photocopying is 5 1/2 cents per copy. It can also be reproduced by the stencil method for an initial preparation cost of $1.38 plus a per-copy cost of one cent. Strictly according to cost, which of the following is the LOWEST number of copies at which it would be more economical to choose the stencil method instead of photo-copying?

    A. 15 B. 30 C. 45 D. 138

14. An employee completed 75% of a clerical assignment in four days.
    How much of it did he complete in the last two days if he finished 3/8 of it in the first two days?

    A. 1/4 B. 3/8 C. 5/8 D. 3/4

15. Seven hundred people are to be scheduled for interviews. If 58% of these 700 people have already been scheduled, how many MORE must be scheduled?

    A. 138 B. 294 C. 406 D. 410

16. In recent years, an average of 35% of the violations reported in any given month have been corrected by the time of a follow-up inspection one month later. Last month, 240 violations were reported, and this month's follow-up inspections show that 93 of them have been corrected.
    How many MORE violations have been corrected than would have been expected, based on the average rate?

    A. 5 B. 9 C. 33 D. 58

17. Suppose that, on a scaled drawing of an office floor plan, 1/2 inch equals 2 feet. An office that is actually 12 feet wide and 17 feet long has which of the following dimensions on this scaled drawing?
    _____ inches wide and _____ inches long.

    A. 3; 4.25 B. 6; 8.5 C. 12; 17 D. 24; 34

Questions 18-21.

In questions 18–21, assume that all arrests fall into two mutually exclusive categories, felonies and misdemeanors. Last week 620 arrests were made in Precinct A, of which 403 were for felonies.

18. The percent of all arrests made in Precinct A last week which were for felonies was _____ percent.

    A. 55 B. 60 C. 65 D. 70

19. If 3/5 of all persons arrested for felonies and 1/4 of all persons arrested for misdemeanors were carrying weapons, then the number of arrests involving persons carrying weapons in Precinct A last week was MOST NEARLY

    A. 135 B. 295 C. 415 D. 525

20. If five times as many men as women were arrested for felonies, and half as many women as men were arrested for misdemeanors, then the number of women arrested in Precinct A last week was APPROXIMATELY

   A. 90	B. 120	C. 140	D. 210

21. If the ratio of arrests made on weekends (Friday through Sunday) to arrests made on weekdays (Monday through Thursday) is 2:1, then the number of arrests made in Precinct A last weekend was approximately

   A. 308	B. 340	C. 372	D. 413

22. The police precincts covering the county receive calls at the average rate of two per minute during the 8 A.M. to 4 P.M. tour, but this rate increases by 50 percent during the 4 P.M. to 12 Midnight tour. However, the initial rate decreases by 50 percent during the 12 Midnight to 8 A.M. tour.
   The number of calls received by the precincts covering the county on this basis in one 24-hour day is

   A. 960	B. 1,440	C. 2,880	D. 3,360

23. If an administrative aide is expected to handle 15 calls per hour and Precinct C averages 840 calls during the 4 P.M. to 12 Midnight tour, then the number of aides needed in Precinct C to handle calls during this tour is

   A. 4	B. 5	C. 6	D. 7

24. If in a group of ten administrative aides four type 40 words per minute, one types 45, two type 50, two type 60, and one types 65, then the average speed in the group is _____ words per minute.

   A. 49	B. 50	C. 51	D. 52

25. An administrative aide works from Midnight to 8 A.M. on a certain day and then is off for 64 hours.
   He is due back at work at

   A. 8 A.M.	B. 12 Noon
   C. 4 P.M.	D. 12 Midnight

KEY (CORRECT ANSWERS)

1. A
2. B
3. C
4. D
5. D

6. B
7. C
8. A
9. A
10. D

11. C
12. A
13. C
14. B
15. B

16. B
17. A
18. C
19. B
20. C

21. D
22. C
23. D
24. A
25. D

SOLUTIONS TO PROBLEMS

1. The distance the 1st car travels = (45)(4/60) = 3 miles. The 2nd car travels 3 3/4 miles in 4 1/2 min. Thus, its speed, in mph, = (3 3/4)(60/4 1/2) = 50

2. Let x = summonses issued in April. Then, (72+60+83+x)/4 = 75 Solving, x = 85

3. Note that 7 patrolmen had 0 absences. Average number of sick days per member = [(1)(8)+(4)(5)+(8)(4)+(5)(3)+(10)(2)+(5)(1)+(7)(0)] ÷ 40 = 100 ÷ 40 = 2 1/2

4. $(7-2-\frac{18}{52}-\frac{11}{52}-\frac{4}{52})(20) \approx 87.3$ man-days, closest to 87.5

5. The car travels 2 1/4 miles in 1 1/2 min. This is equivalent to (2 1/4)(60/1 1/2) = 90 mph.

6. There were 21,500 - 550 - 2230 = 18,720 cars. Total income = (18,720)($1) + ($2)(2230) + ($4)(550) = $25,380

7. Distance = 100 + (100)(.90) + (100)(.90)(.90) + (100)(.90)(.90)(.90) = 343.9 ≈ 344 ft.

8. $250 - $90 = $160, and ($160)(.40) = $64. After buying the jacket and trousers, he has $250 - $90 - $64 = $96 left.
   He will be short of the overcoat's price by ($120-$96) ÷ $120 = 20%

9. 9000 ÷ 30 = 300 gallons, 9000 ÷ 15 = 600 gallons. The savings = (600-300)($3.75) = $1,125

10. (14,200-12,800) ÷ (34,750-32,300) ≈ 57%

11. The 1st office handles 600 applicants while the 2nd office handles 300 applicants. The total number of permits = (.60)(600) + (.40X300) = 480

12. 2773 - (5)(301) - 1032 = 236 calls

13. Let x = number of copies where the two methods are equal in cost. Then, .055x = $1.38 + .01x. Solving, x = 30 2/3. Thus, 31 copies would be the lowest number so that the stencil method is more economical. (For 31 copies, stencil method costs $1.69, whereas the photocopying method costs $1.705.)

14. $.75 - \frac{3}{8} = \frac{3}{4} - \frac{3}{8} = \frac{3}{8}$

15. (100%-58%)(700) = (.42X700) = 294

16. 93 - (.35)(240) = 9

17. (12/2)(1/2") = 3" and (17/2)(1/2") = 4.25"

18. 403/620 = 65% for felonies

19. (3/5)(403) + (1/4)(217) = 296.05, closest to 295

20. Let x = number of women arrested for felonies and let y = number of women arrested for misdemeanors. Then, x + 5x = 403 and y + 2y = 217. Solving, x = 67.1$\overline{6}$ and y = 72.$\overline{3}$. Thus, x + y = 140

21. Let x = arrest on weekends, 1/2x = those during week. 3/2x = 620, so x ≈ 413

22. (2)(480 min.) + (3)(480 min.) + (1)(480 min.) = 2880 calls

23. 4 PM to Midnight = 8 hrs. Then, one aide can handle (15)(8) = 120 calls during this shift. Thus, 840 ÷ 120 = 7 aides are needed.

24. Average speed in wpm = [(4)(40)+(1)(45)+(2)(50)+(2)(60)+(1)(65)] ÷ 10 = 49

25. 8 AM + 64 hrs. = 8 AM + 2 days + 16 hrs., which would be 12 Midnight

TEST 2

DIRECTIONS: Each question or incomplete statement is followed by several suggested answers or completions. Select the one that BEST answers the question or completes the statement. *PRINT THE LETTER OF THE CORRECT ANSWER IN THE SPACE AT THE RIGHT.*

1. If a security officer gets $10.82 per hour and $16.26 per hour for overtime work, his GROSS salary for a week in which he works 5 hours over his regular 40 hours is

   A. $433.60   B. $487.80   C. $514.10   D. $650.40

   1.____

2. It takes 2 minutes 45 seconds for a security officer to travel to his first clock station, 3 minutes to get to the second, 2 minutes to get to the third, 5 1/2 minutes to get to the fourth, and 4 minutes 15 seconds to get from the fourth back to the starting point. Neglecting the time spent at each clock station, the TOTAL time needed to make one round tour is_____ minutes _____seconds.

   A. 16; 45   B. 17; 15   C. 17; 30   D. 18; 0

   2.____

3. The log book of a security officer stationed at an entry gate shows 47 entries in two hours.
   At this rate, the number of entries in eight hours is

   A. 108   B. 168   C. 188   D. 376

   3.____

4. A truck driver leaving Authority property has a requisition form showing 14 cartons of pencils, 12 cartons of pens, 27 cartons of envelopes, and 39 cartons of writing pads.
   If an actual count of the cartons on the truck shows only 77 cartons, the number of cartons missing is

   A. 15   B. 14   C. 12   D. 5

   4.____

5. If a certain aide takes one hour to type 2 accident reports or 6 missing persons reports, then the length of time he will require to finish 7 accident reports and 15 missing persons reports is _____hours _____ minutes.

   A. 6; 0   B. 6; 30   C. 8; 0   D. 8; 40

   5.____

6. If one administrative aide can alphabetize 320 reports per hour and another can do 280 per hour, then the number of reports that both could alphabetize during an 8-hour tour is

   A. 4,800   B. 5,200   C. 5,400   D. 5,700

   6.____

7. If 1,000 candidates applied for administrative aide, and out of those applying 7/8 appear for the written test, and out of those who take the written test 66 2/3 percent pass it, and out of those who pass the written test 85 percent pass the medical exam, then the number of candidates still eligible to become administrative aides will be about

   A. 245   B. 495   C. 585   D. 745

   7.____

8. If the number of murders in the city in 2005 was 415, and the number of murders has increased by 8 percent each year since that year, then in 2008 we would expect the number of murders to be about

   A. 484   B. 523   C. 548   D. 565

   8.____

9. If a person reported missing on April 15 was found murdered on July 4, how many days was he missing? (Include April 15 but NOT July 4 in the total.)

   A. 76   B. 80   C. 82   D. 84

10. Suppose that a pile of 96 file cards measures one inch in height and that it takes you half an hour to file these cards away.
    If you are given three piles of cards which measure 2 1/2 inches high, 1 3/4 inches high, and 3 3/8 inches high, respectively, the time it would take to file the cards is MOST NEARLY _____ hours and _____ minutes.

    A. 2; 30   B. 3; 50   C. 6; 45   D. 8; 15

11. Suppose that police expenses in the city in a certain year amounted to 7.5% of total expenses.
    In indicating this percentage on a *pie* or circular chart, which is 360°, the size of the angle between the two radiuses would be MOST NEARLY

    A. 3.7°   B. 7.5°   C. 27°   D. 54°

12. Suppose that in police precinct A, where there are 4,180 children, 627 children entered a contest sponsored by the Police Community Relations Bureau. In precinct B, where there were 7,840 children, 1,960 children entered the contest.
    The total percentage of all children in both precincts who entered the contest amounted to MOST NEARLY

    A. 19.5%   B. 20%   C. 21.5%   D. 22.5%

13. If Circle A represents Police Administrative Aides (PAA's) who scored above 85 on a PAA test and Circle B represents PAA's who scored above 85 on a Senior PAA test, then the diagram shown at the right means that

    A. no PAA who scored above 85 on a PAA test scored above 85 on the Senior PAA test
    B. the majority of PAA's who scored above 85 on a PAA test scored above 85 on the Senior PAA test
    C. there were some PAA's who did not take the Senior PAA test
    D. some PAA's who scored above 85 on a PAA test scored above 85 on the Senior PAA test

14. Suppose that in 1844 the city had a population of 550,000 and a police force of 200, and that in 1992 the city had a population of 8,000,000 and a police force of 32,000.
    If the ratio of police to population in 1992 is compared with the same ratio in 1844, what is the resulting relationship of the 1992 ratio to the 1844 ratio?

    A. 160:11   B. 160:1   C. 16:1   D. 11:1

15. A squad of patrolmen assigned to enforce a new parking regulation in a particular area issued tag summonses on a particular day as follows: four patrolmen issued 16 summonses each, three issued 19 each, one issued 22, seven issued 25 each, eleven issued 28 each, ten issued 30 each, two issued 36 each, one issued 41; and three issued 45 each.
The average number of summonses issued by a member of this squad was MOST NEARLY

   A. 6.2   B. 17.2   C. 21.0   D. 27.9

16. A water storage tank is 75 feet long and 30 feet wide and has a depth of 6 1/2 feet. Each cubic foot of the tank holds 9 1/2 gallons.
The TOTAL capacity of the tank is _____ gallons.

   A. 73,125 1/2   B. 131,625   C. 138,937 1/2   D. 146,250

17. The prices of admission to a PAL entertainment were $1.25 each for adults and $.50 for children. The turnstile at the entrance showed that 358 persons entered, and the gate receipts were $313.25.
The number of children who attended was

   A. 170   B. 175   C. 179   D. 183

18. A patrol car travels six times as fast as a bicycle.
If the patrol car goes 168 miles in two hours less time than the bicycle requires to go 42 miles, their respective rates of speed are_____ miles per hour.

   A. 36 and 6   B. 42 and 7   C. 63 and 10 1/2   D. 126 and 21

19. A man received an inheritance of $8,000 and wanted to invest it so that it would produce an annual income sufficient to pay his rent of $40 a month.
In order to do this, he will have to receive interest or dividends at the rate of _____% per annum.

   A. 3   B. 4   C. 5 3/4   D. 6

20. If the price of a bus ticket varies DIRECTLY as the mileage involved and a ticket to travel 135 miles costs $29.70, a ticket for a 30-mile trip will cost

   A. $15.20   B. $13.40   C. $6.60   D. $2.20

21. A man owed a debt of $580. After a first payment of $10, he agreed to pay the balance by monthly payments in which each payment after this first would be $2 more than that of the preceding month.
If no interest charge is made, he will have to make, including the first payment, a total of _____ monthly payments.

   A. 16   B. 20   C. 24   D. 28

22. The written test of a civil service examination has a weight of 30, the oral test a weight of 20, experience a weight of 20, and the physical test a weight of 30.
A candidate received ratings of 76 on the written test, 84 on the oral, and 80 for experience.
In order to attain an average of 85 on the examination, his rating on the physical test must be

   A. 86   B. 90   C. 94   D. 98

23. A family has an income of $320 per week. It spends 22% of this amount for rent, 36% for food, 16% for clothing, and 12% for additional household expenses. After meeting these expenses, 50% of the balance is deposited in the bank.
The amount deposited weekly is

   A. $22.40   B. $36.60   C. $44.80   D. $52.00

24. Upon retirement last July, a patrolman bought a farm of 64 acres for $1800 per acre. He made a downpayment of $61,200 and agreed to pay the balance in installments of $750 a month commencing on August 1, 1993. Disregarding interest, he will make his LAST payment on

   A. July 1999   B. August 2001
   C. January 2003   D. April 2006

25. 40% of those who commit a particular crime are subsequently arrested and convicted; 75% of these convicted receive sentences of 10 years or more.
Assuming that those arrested for the first time serve less than 10 years, the percentage of those committing this crime who receive sentences of ten years or more is MOST NEARLY

   A. 20%   B. 30%   C. 40%   D. 50%

KEY (CORRECT ANSWERS)

1.	C	11.	C
2.	C	12.	C
3.	C	13.	D
4.	A	14.	D
5.	A	15.	D
6.	A	16.	C
7.	B	17.	C
8.	B	18.	B
9.	B	19.	D
10.	B	20.	C

21. B
22. D
23. A
24. A
25. B

SOLUTIONS TO PROBLEMS

1. Gross salary = (40)($10.82) + (5)($16.26) = $514.10

2. 2 min. 45 sec. + 3 min. + 2 min. + 5 min. 30 sec. + 4 min. 15 sec. = 16 min. 90 sec. = 17 min. 30 sec.

3. (47)(8/2) = 188 entries

4. 14 + 12 + 27 + 39 - 77 = 15 cartons missing

5. (1 hr.)(7/2) + (1 hr.)(15/6) = 6 hrs. 0 min.

6. 8)(320+280) = 4800 reports

7. Number of eligibles = $(1000)(\frac{7}{8})(\frac{2}{3})(\frac{85}{100}) \approx 495$ (Actual answer is 495.8$\bar{3}$)

8. Number of murders in 2008 = $(415)(1.08)^3 \approx 523$

9. Number of days in April, May, June, July = 16, 31, 30, 3 Total is 80 days

10. Total inches = 7 5/8 . Then, (7 5/8)(1/2 hr.) = 3 3/16 hrs. $\approx$ 3 hrs. 50 min.

11. (360°)(.075) = 27°

12. (627+1960)7(4180+7840) = 2587/12,020 $\approx$ 21.5%

13. Since the circles overlap, some PAA's scored above 85 on both a PAA test and a Senior PAA test.

14. 32,000/8,000,000 = .004; 200/550,000 = 1/2750 Then, $.004; \frac{1}{2750} = (\frac{1}{25})(\frac{2750}{1}) = 11:1$

15. [(4)(16)+(3)(19)+(1)(22)+(7)(25)+(11)(28)+(10)(30)+(2)(36) +(1)(41)+(3)(45)] $\div$ 42 $\approx$ 27.9

16. Total capacity = (9 1/2)(75)(30)(6 1/2) = 138,937 1/2 gallons

17. Let x = number of children, 358-x = number of adults. Then, $.50x + ($1.25)(358-x) = $313.25. Simplifying, -.75x + $447.50 = $313.25. Solving, x = 179

18. Let x = rate of patrol car (in mph), 1/6x = rate of bike (in mph). Then, 168/x + 2 = 42/1/6x. Simplifying, 168 + 2x = 252. Solving, x = 42 and 1/6x = 7

19. ($40)(12) = $480. Then, $480/$8000 = 6%

20. Cost = (30/135)($29.70) = $6.60

21. This is an arithmetic series $10 + $12 + $14 + ... The formula for a sum of n terms is $S = n/2[2a+(n-1)d]$, where a = 1st term, d = difference between terms. Thus, $580 = n/2[20+(n-1)($2)]$. Simplifying, $580 = n(n+4)$. Then, $n^2 + 9n - 580 = 0$. This becomes $(n+29)(n-20) = 0$. Ignoring the negative answer, n = 20

22. Let x = rating on physical test. Then, $(76)(.30)+(84)(.20)+ (80)(.20) + (x)(.30) = 85$. Solving, x = 98

23. 100% - 22% - 36% - 16% - 12% = 14%. This means that $(1/2)(.14)($320) = 22.40 is deposited in the bank.

24. $(64)($1800) = $115,200$. Then, $115,200 - $61,200 = $54,000$ to be paid off in installments of $750 per month. So, $54,000 \div $750 = 72$ months = 6 yrs. If August 1993 is his first payment, July 1999 is his last payment.

25. $(.40)(.75) = .30 = 30\%$

TEST 3

DIRECTIONS: Each question or incomplete statement is followed by several suggested answers or completions. Select the one that BEST answers the question or completes the statement. *PRINT THE LETTER OF THE CORRECT ANSWER IN THE SPACE AT THE RIGHT.*

1. During the first nine months of 2008, an officer spent an average of $270 a month. In October and November, he spent an average of $315 a month. In December, he spent $385.
   His average monthly spending during the year was MOST NEARLY

   A. $254 B. $287 C. $323 D. $3,000

2. In 2005, there were 8,270 arrests in a certain city. In 2006, the number of arrests increased by 12 1/2%. In 2007, the number of arrests decreased 5% from the 2006 figures. The number of arrests in 2007 was MOST NEARLY

   A. 8,840 B. 9,770 C. 6,870 D. 7,600

3. Assume that parking space is to be provided for 25% of the tenants in a new housing development. The project will have five 6-story buildings, having seven tenants on each floor, and eight 11-story buildings, having eight tenants on each floor.
   The number of parking spaces needed is MOST NEARLY

   A. 215 B. 230 C. 700 D. 895

4. A stolen vehicle traveling at 60 miles per hour passes by a police car, which is standing still with the engine running. The police car immediately starts out in pursuit, and one minute later, having covered a distance of half a mile, it reaches a speed of 90 miles per hour and continues at this speed.
   In how many minutes after the stolen vehicle passes the police car will the police car overtake it? _____ minutes.

   A. 1 B. 1 1/2 C. 2 D. 3

5. A police officer found his 42-hour work week was divided as follows: 1/6 of his time in investigating incidents on his patrol post, 1/2 of his time patrolling his post, and 1/8 of his time in special traffic duty. The rest of his time was devoted to assignments at precinct headquarters.
   The percentage of his work week which was spent at precinct headquarters is MOST NEARLY

   A. 10% B. 15% C. 20% D. 25%

6. During the year, the Department of Sanitation towed away 8,430 cars which were abandoned or illegally parked on city streets.
   If the value of the abandoned cars was $10,382,000 and that of the illegally parked cars was $62,348,000, then the average value of one of the towed away cars was MOST NEARLY

   A. $4,000 B. $7,200 C. $8,600 D. $11,000

7. Two percent of all school children are problem children. Some 80% of these problem children become delinquents, and about 80% of the delinquent children become criminals. If the school population is 1,000,000 children, the number of this group who will eventually become criminals, according to this analysis, is

   A. 12,800   B. 1,280   C. 640   D. 128

8. A patrol car began a trip with 12 gallons of gasoline in the tank and ended with 7 1/2 gallons. The car traveled 17.3 miles for each gallon of gasoline. During the trip, gasoline was bought for $27.84 at a cost of $3.48 per gallon.
   The total number of miles traveled during this trip was MOST NEARLY

   A. 79   B. 196   C. 216   D. 229

9. A radio motor patrol car has to travel a distance of 15 miles in an emergency.
   If it does the first two-thirds of the distance at 40 mph and the last third at 60 mph, the total number of minutes required for the entire run is MOST NEARLY

   A. 15   B. 20   C. 22 1/2   D. 25

10. A patrol car had 11 1/2 gallons of gasoline at the beginning of a trip of 196 miles and 5 1/2 gallons at the end of the trip. During the trip, gasoline was bought for $21.70 at a cost of $4.65 per gallon.
    The average number of miles driven per gallon of gasoline is MOST NEARLY

    A. 14   B. 14.5   C. 15   D. 15.5

11. There are 15 patrolmen assigned to a certain operation. One-third earn $21,000 per year, three earn $22,050 per year, one earns $24,675 per year, and the rest earn $27,905 per year.
    The average annual salary of these patrolmen is MOST NEARLY

    A. $23,750   B. $24,000   C. $24,250   D. $24,500

12. In 1991, the cost of patrol car maintenance and repair was $2,500 more than in 1990, representing an increase of 10%.
    The cost of patrol car maintenance and repair in 1991 was MOST NEARLY

    A. $2,750   B. $22,500   C. $25,000   D. $27,500

13. A police precinct has an assigned strength of 180 men. Of this number, 25% are not available for duty due to illness, vacations, and other reasons. Of those who are available for duty, 1/3 are assigned outside of the precinct for special emergency duty.
    The ACTUAL available strength of the precinct in terms of men immediately available for precinct duty is

    A. 45   B. 60   C. 90   D. 135

14. Five police officers are taking target practice. The number of rounds fired by each and the percentage of perfect shots is as follows:

Officer	Rounds Fired	Perfect Shots
R	80	30%
S	70	40%
T	75	60%
U	92	25%
V	96	66-2/3%

    The average number of perfect shots fired by them is MOST NEARLY
    A. A. 30   B. 36   C. 42   D. 80

15. A dozen 5-gallon cans of paint weigh 494 pounds. Each can, when empty, weighs 3 pounds.
    The weight of one gallon of paint is MOST NEARLY ____ lbs.

    A. 5   B. 6 1/2   C. 7 1/2   D. 8

16. Assume that a parking space for six cars is to be outlined with white paint. The total area to be outlined is 24 feet by 40 feet, and the space for each car, also marked off by white lines, is to be 8 feet by 20 feet. The total length of white lines to be painted is MOST NEARLY _____ feet.

    A. 64   B. 128   C. 184   D. 232

17. A police car is ordered to report to the scene of a crime 5 miles away.
    If the car travels at an average rate of 40 miles per hour, the length of time it will take to reach its destination is MOST NEARLY _____ minutes.

    A. 3   B. 7   C. 10   D. 13

18. A block has metered parking for 19 cars from 7 A.M. to 9 P.M. at a charge of 10 cents per hour.
    Assuming that each car that is parked remains for a full hour and that on an average, for each hour of parking, there is a vacancy of five minutes for each meter, the amount of revenue from the meters for a day will be MOST NEARLY

    A. $10   B. $15   C. $20   D. $25

19. The standard formula for the stopping distance of a car with all four wheels locked is:

    $$S = \frac{V \text{ times } V}{30W}$$

    where S is the stopping distance in feet, V the speed of the car in miles per hour at the moment the brakes are applied, and W is a number which depends on the friction between the tires and the road.
    If the speed of a car is 50 miles per hour and W is equal to 5/3, the stopping distance will be MOST NEARLY _____ feet.

    A. 30   B. 40   C. 50   D. 60

20. The radiator of a police car contains 20 quarts of a mixture consisting of 80% water and 20% anti-freeze compound. Assume that you have been ordered to draw off some of the mixture and add pure anti-freeze compound until the mixture is 75% water and 25% anti-freeze compound.
    The number of quarts of the mixture which should be removed is MOST NEARLY

    A. 2   B. 3   C. 4   D. 5

KEY (CORRECT ANSWERS)

1. B
2. A
3. B
4. C
5. C

6. C
7. A
8. C
9. B
10. C

11. C
12. D
13. C
14. B
15. C

16. D
17. B
18. D
19. C
20. A

SOLUTIONS TO PROBLEMS

1. Average = [($270)(9)+($315)(2)+($385)(1)] ÷ 12 ≈ $287

2. Number of arrests in 2007 = (8270)(1.125)(.95) ≈ 8839, closest to 8840

3. Number of parking spaces = (.25)[(5)(6)(7)+(8)(11)(8)] = (.25)(914) = 228.5 ≈ 230

4. After 1 min., the stolen car has traveled 1 mile, while the police car has traveled 1/2 mile. Let x = additional minutes needed for the police car to catch up to the stolen vehicle. Using (rate)(time) = distance and the fact that the police car will travel 1/2 extra mile, (1 mi./min)(x) = (1 1/2 mi./min.)(x) - 1/2. Solving, x = 1. Total time = 2 min.

5. $1 - \frac{1}{6} - \frac{1}{2} - \frac{1}{8} = \frac{5}{24} \approx 20\%$

6. ($10,382,000+$62,348,000)/8430 ≈ $8628, which is closest to $8600

7. (1,000,000)(.02)(.80)(.80) = 12,800

8. Total miles = (17.3)(12-7 1/2) + (17.3)($27.84/$3.48) = 77.85 + 138.4 ≈ 216

9. Total min. = (10)(60/40) + (5)(60/60) = 20

10. Total miles = 196. Number of gallons used = (11 1/2-5 1/2) + ($21.70/$4.65) = 13. Avg. mil/gallon = 196 ÷ 13 ≈ 15

11. Average annual salary = [(5)($21,000)+(3)($22,050)+(1)($24,675) +(6)($27,905)] ÷ 15 = $24,217, closest to $24,250

12. Cost in 1991 = $2500 + $2500/.10 = $27,500

13. Number of men actually available for precinct duty = (180)(.75X2/3) = 90

14. Avg. number of perfect shots = [(80)(.30)+(70)(.40)+(75)(.60) +(92)(.25)+(96)(2/3)] ÷ 5 = 36.8, closest to 36

15. Each full can weighs 494 ÷ 12 = 41 1/6 lbs. The weight of 5 gallons = 41 1/6 - 3 = 38 1/6 lbs. So, one gallon of paint weighs 38 1/6 ÷ 5 ≈ 7.63, closest to 7 1/2 lbs.

16. Length of vertical lines = (3)(24') = 72 ft.
    Length of horizontal lines = (4)(40) = 160 ft.
    Total length of white lines = 232 ft.

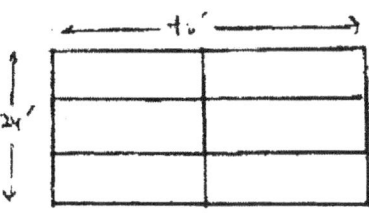

17. 40 mi/hr = 2/3 mi/min. Thus, a distance of 5 miles requires $5 \div \frac{2}{3} = 7\frac{1}{2} \approx 7$ min.

18. Each meter will produce revenue from 13 cars, due to the 5 min. vacancy between cars leaving and parking. Amount of revenue for all meters = (19)(13)(.10) = $24.70 ≈ $25

19. S = (50)(50)/(30)(5/3) = 50 ft.

20. Let x = amount of mixture removed and also amount of anti-freeze added back in. When x quarts of the mixture are removed, 20-x quarts are left, of which 4-.20x is antifreeze. After adding back x quarts of antifreeze, we have 4-.20x+x quarts of antifreeze and 20 quarts of mixture. Then, (4+.80x)/20 = .25. Solving, x = 1.25, closest to 2 quarts.

www.ingramcontent.com/pod-product-compliance
Lightning Source LLC
Chambersburg PA
CBHW082041300426
44117CB00015B/2561